Algrove Publishing Limited
1090 Morrison Drive
Ottawa, Ontario
Canada K2H 1C2

Canadian Cataloguing in Publication Data

Brown, Annora, 1899-1987
    Old man's garden

(Classic reprint series)
Originally published: Toronto : J.M. Dent & Sons, 1954.
Includes index.
ISBN 1-894572-12-2

        1. Botany--Canada, Western.   2. Ethnobotany--Canada, Western.   I. Title.
II. Series: Classic reprint series (Ottawa, Ont.)

QK201.B8 2000   581.9712   C00-900942-6

Printed in Canada
#11000

Publisher's Note

The only thing less likely to succeed in publishing than a limited interest book is one that is also regional in nature. Regardless, Annora Brown's 1954 book about Western Canadian plants deserves a second life in print because of its innate charm and the wonderful botanical and historical minutiae it contains. As she admits in her introduction, it is "…a book of gossip about the flowers of the west." Would that there were a book of equally good gossip about the flowers of the east.

Leonard G. Lee, Publisher
Ottawa
August, 2000

OLD MAN'S GARDEN

ANNORA BROWN

OLD MAN'S GARDEN

WITH ILLUSTRATIONS BY THE AUTHOR

J. M. DENT & SONS (CANADA) LIMITED
Toronto · Vancouver

CONTENTS

INTRODUCTION

This is a book of gossip about the flowers of the west. Its purpose is to gather under one cover some of the legend and lore that is to be found lying about in odd corners, not easily available to those whose reading time is limited. It has been no more possible to mention all the flowers of the country than it would be to mention all one's friends in an evening's chat; but it is hoped that the bits of gossip included will change the flowers from strange botanical specimens to friends.

Native western flowers, though dethroned now by scentless, sophisticated hybrids from the hot-house, have played their roles in many a solemn ceremony. Long before the white man first appeared, the sage and sweet grass were sacred flowers; the camas, the bread root, and the arrowhead furnished food; the saskatoon and cow parsnip had ceremonial roles to play.

It seems appropriate, in a work of this kind, that the first acknowledgement should be made to the original naturalists and poets of the country, the Indians who have added so greatly to the world's collection of beautiful thoughts; and that the second should be made to those early travellers, who, in spite of all the trials of life in a new country, found time and courage to record what they saw and heard of the flowers around them.

Across the west, following the earliest of travellers from the mouth of the Mississippi in the south to the Athabasca Lake in the north, spread a thin veneer of French-Canadian and half breed population. The *voyageurs* and *engagés* of the great fur companies added their quota of familiar names and superstitions to the flowers in their paths.

Soon the west was overrun with settlers of all nationalities, immigrants who followed the explorers and brought stories from the old land to add to the new world culture—stories of ghosts and witches and strange mediaeval superstitions, as well as stories of the first dawn of the science of botany.

My information has been obtained by living amongst the old timers who remember the days when native plants were a necessary part of daily life, and by digging into the journals and writings of the early explorers and settlers, as follows: *The North West Passage by Land,* published jointly by Walter Butler Cheadle and Lord Milton, London, 1865 (new edition, Ottawa, 1931); *Journey to the Shores of the Polar Sea,* by Capt. John Franklin, R.N.; *A Journal of Voyages and Travels in the Interior of North America,* by Daniel W. Harmon, Andover, U.S.A., 1820 (reprinted New York, 1903); *The Original Journals of the Lewis and Clark Expedition,* edited by R. G. Thwaites, 1905; Alexander Mackenzie's *Voyages from Montreal on the River St. Lawrence through the continent of North America to the frozen and Pacific Oceans in the years 1789 and 1793,* London, 1801 (reprinted Toronto, 1927, in Volume III of *Master Works of Canadian Authors,* John W. Garvin, editor); Captain John Palliser's *Report,* issued in the British Parliamentary Papers for 1863.

Other works used for reference include: John Adams, *A Survey of Canadian Plants in Relation to their Environment* (Dominion of Canada, Department of Agriculture, Bulletin No. 58); Nina Marshall, *Mosses and Lichens;* Walter McClintock, *Old North Trail;* C. F. Saunders, *Useful Plants of the United States and Canada* and *Western Wild Flowers and their Stories;* Chapters by W. J. Showalter on plant life and flower biographies in *The Book of Wild Flowers,* National Geographic Society, 1924; J. D. Smith, *Weeds of Alberta* (Province of Alberta, Department of Agriculture); and C. H. Sternberg, *Hunting Dinosaurs in the Bad Lands.*

The scientific names used are generally the ones chosen by P. A. Rydberg in his *Flora of the Rocky Mountains and Adjacent Plains* which is the only botany easily obtainable in which all the species are included.

ANNORA BROWN

OLD MAN'S GARDEN

I. Wi-Suk-i-tshak

OLD MAN

OLD MAN is a mythical being common to all the Indian tribes of the prairie, a character familiar under various names, Glooscap, Coyote Man, Rabbit, or Raven, in all parts of the continent. Most of the legends of him included here are familiar stories of the foothill regions.

All the rarest and most beautiful of the legends of the prairie Indians relate to the Sun, his wife the Moon and their son the Morning Star. But heavenly bodies are remote and the human heart craves something more tangible, more like itself, on which to hang such stories as the story of the Creation. So Old Man — 'Wi-suk-i-tshak' — part sun, part god, part man, came into being.

Old Man created the World.

At one time the sun came out of his lodge at dawn to pace across an empty sky. Below him was an empty earth. There were no mountains, nor hills, nor prairies, but only a great water. Across the endless surface of this water Old Man and the animals floated about on a raft looking for land, but as far as they could see in any direction was emptiness — a sea of water below, a sea of air above. Search as they might they could not find even the smallest island.

At last Old Man said to the loon, "Dive down as far as you can. See if you can find some mud and I will make some land." So the loon dived into the water but could find no mud. Then the muskrat tried, and the otter, but the water was too deep and they could find no mud. Then the beaver slid off the raft and was gone for a long time. He was gone so long that the animals on the raft thought that they would never see him again. But at last Old Man saw him floating on the surface of the water too exhausted to climb back onto the raft.

Old Man lifted him up, unconscious, from the water and there, clutched in his paw, was a little ball of mud.

Old Man took the mud and he made the earth. He piled up great heaps of mud and said, "You will be the Backbone." And so he made the mountains. He made Chief Mountain and the Crow's Nest, the Three Sisters and Devil's Peak and all the other peaks that are a part of the Great Backbone, and he made the level prairie. He created the land which stretches from the Athabasca River in the north to the Missouri in the south, from the Great Divide on the west far out to the eastern prairies.

At first the world was bleak and bare, high walls of grey rock and wastes of desert sand. But Old Man covered them with grass, and with flowers and trees. He put birds in the sky and animals on the land. He made Man and taught him to live with the aid of the flowers and animals.

All these beautiful and kindly things are attributed to Old Man, but there are other stories about him too, stories that show him as mean and vicious, a mere buffoon and a simpleton, foolish enough to be tricked by the very creatures he made. In other words he was just a creature, a name on which to hang the stories of the country.

THE GARDEN

It is with Old Man's Garden that we are here concerned; the garden that, from the Moon-of-heavy-snows until the Moon-when-the-leaves-turn-yellow, provides a continual round of interest and entertainment. It is the stupendousness of the garden and the variety that is most amazing. No puny efforts nor specializing in a few varieties in Old Man's Garden! He has flowers of the open prairie of course, and flowers of the moist dark forests, flowers that grow at low altitudes having their full measure of summer sun, and flowers that cling to dizzy mountain heights, having but a few weeks for growing season, being covered with snow at times even in July and August.

Perhaps his Rock Garden is the greatest of his undertakings. With aeons of time at his disposal, he spared no efforts to have this garden perfect and so he has given us the unique possession of a garden where one may climb from summer back to spring and even to the very edge of winter in the short space of a single hour.

He did a bit of experimenting in swamps, laying out a few thousand acres in sphagnum bogs of every degree of progress from open water to those which sway but slightly to the tread.

He tried some desert, bringing drought-loving flowers from the south, experimenting in forms of cactus and sage and other denizens of the desert land.

Here, a thousand miles from the sea, he even tried a miniature sea shore; for along the edge of prairie lakes which have no outlet is a crusting of alkali on which grow plants found elsewhere only on the sea-shore — samphire, sea crowfoot, sea milkwort and others.

Collecting, examining and classifying form only a part of knowing the plants of this varied locale. Their story and legend are vital to the history of the country where they grow and of the trail that has been blazed in so short a time from primitive childhood to civilized manhood. Old Man created all this variety for the use and pleasure of his people, and we who have inherited it take full measure of enjoyment from its wonder.

II. Trail Blazers

"On May 3rd, 1858, the Phlox hoodii bloomed
on the prairie about Fort Carlton."
Palliser's Report

FORT CARLTON was the last small outpost of civilization on the Saskatchewan River, the jumping off place for travellers to the great rivers of the north which had been known for nearly half a century.

Away to the south, on the Missouri River, was another outpost, Bismark, an excited, bustling, fur trading centre. Even then plans were being laid for the building of a sternwheeler, the *Chippewa,* that was to push its way up the Missouri to give birth to another frontier town, Fort Benton, in what is now the very heart of Montana.

To the westward of these two outposts was a wilderness of prairie and mountain, penetrated as yet by only two or three lone white men. Peter Fidler of the Hudson's Bay Company had once caught a glimpse of the northern silhouette of Chief Mountain. David Thompson, of the North West Company, had spent a winter with the Piegans and Sir George Simpson had penetrated the mountains to Lake Minnewanka, but now their footprints were lost again in the wilderness of plains. On the banks of the Bow River, just west of what is now the city of Calgary, stood two gaunt chimneys of an old fort, abandoned by the Hudson's Bay Company because of the ferocity of the Indians. This was the only trace of the white man in the whole vast territory.

But in the spring of 1858 the blooms of the prairie were crushed and trampled under the great wooden wheels of Red River carts as Captain Palliser and his party set out to blaze a trail for civilization across this wilderness. Theirs was the task — no small one — of exploring the Rocky Mountains, the foothills and the plains, from the Athabasca River in the north to the International Boundary in the south, of taking meridian observations, of mapping the country, recording the weather and of finding a passage through the mountains to the western sea.

The man who, amidst all these gigantic undertakings, had time to note that the *Phlox hoodii* was in bloom on May 3rd was Monsieur Bourgeau, the botanist of the expedition. That the position of botanist was no secondary one is indicated by more than one entry in the journals to the effect that the entire party was delayed while Monsieur Bourgeau dried and preserved his specimens. And since he could not be in every place at once, his companions helped him with his collecting. Sir James Hector brought specimens with him from the Kicking Horse Pass and, though on the very verge of starvation, never failed to note in his diary any change of vegetation or common flower. He named a mountain Bourgeau, in honour of the botanist, just west of Banff. Blakiston also hunted specimens for Bourgeau at Waterton Lakes, returning with many that the botanist had not so far found.

The specimens they collected were sent to the famous botanist Sir William Hooker and now form a part of the greatest dried plant collection in the world, which is at the Royal Gardens at Kew. These specimens were of three types: first, plant specimens for preservation in herbaria; second, seeds and roots for culture in botanical gardens; third, vegetable products used by the Indians. Twelve specimens of each variety were sent, all of which were labelled and named before their issue from Kew to various public collections. It was then that many hitherto unnamed species received scientific recognition, for out of the 819 specimens sent, there were 62 species which were new in spite of all the enthusiasm of botanists since the beginning of the century for new discoveries in the west.

But Monsieur Bourgeau was not by any means the only collector of western plants, nor even the first. Alexander Mackenzie, who, in 1789 made his daring trip up the river which now bears his name and in 1793 made such a spectacular dash alone across the mountains to the Pacific, says with regret:

> "I could not stop to dig into the earth over whose surface I was compelled to pass with rapid steps; nor could I turn aside to collect the plants which nature might have scattered on the way, when my thoughts were so anxiously employed in making provision for the day that was passing over me."

When we remember the difficulties and dangers that dogged his every step, we marvel that he was able to record so much. Carrying his full share of the weight of the packs, taking all the responsibility, bolstering up the courage of his men, sitting up nights to prevent his guide from escaping, or taking the guide and all the undesirable company that had collected in his mangy robe to bed with him, so that he might keep his hand on him, Mackenzie still found time to note in his journal many of the flowers he passed on the way and the source and method of preparation of many of the vegetable foods used by the natives.

In the years 1804 to 1806, a party under the command of Captains Lewis and Clark followed the Missouri River to its source, crossed the mountains and reached the coast by way of the Columbia River. Captain Lewis was the botanist and recorded many interesting facts about the flowers and plants he found. Unfortunately the collection he made on his westward trip was lost and so only 150 specimens were sent back to the east. The plants of our territory, therefore, which he sent east were almost entirely those to be found in bloom at mid-summer. His specimens found their way to the famous botanist Frederick Pursh, who first gave them scientific names and wrote about them in his book *North American Wild Flowers*. Many of these flowers we now call familiarly by the names which Pursh first chose for them at his desk in New York. More often, however, their story is simply recorded in their scientific names.

One of the best known stories of exploration on the continent is the story of Sir John Franklin who went three times into the Arctic and on the third journey was lost. Nearly forty relief expeditions were sent in search of him, but not until thirty years later were the remains of his party found. With him on his first two trips went Sir John Richardson, Scottish surgeon and naturalist. He later conducted a search expedition for the lost Franklin. During all the incredible hardship suffered by all members of the party, Dr. Richardson never forgot his mission, nor neglected his specimens. The letters *rich.* after many of our best known species tell the story of his careful work, while other members of the party are commemorated by specific names.

Thomas Drummond, also a native of Scotland, was assistant to Sir John Richardson on the second expedition. In 1825 Franklin and Richardson wintered at Great Bear Lake and sent Drummond on a one man botanical trip to the Rockies. Drummond spent the winter alone on the Berland River about fifty miles straight north of the town of Jasper. He complained that the winter was long as he had no books and nothing could be done in the way of collecting specimens. However, his biographer says that his collections altogether amounted to about fifteen hundred species of plants, one hundred and fifty birds, fifty quadrupeds and a considerable number of insects.

David Douglas, sent out to the Pacific coast by the Royal Horticultural Society of London for the purpose of collecting new specimens for old world gardens, although he never actually reached our territory, came very close both in Oregon and on the head waters of the northern branch of the Columbia. He is responsible for the naming of many of our flower species since flowers know no artificial boundaries and he found many of them in adjoining regions.

In 1862 Dr. Cheadle and Lord Milton crossed the prairies for their own pleasure but Dr. Cheadle, being interested in such things, made a careful collection of all the flowers he passed on the way. Unfortunately, as they made their way across a mountain torrent on the other side of the Yellowhead Pass, two horses were carried down the river, one to be lost forever over the falls, the other to remain submerged so long that eveything in the pack, including the precious plant collections, was ruined by the muddy waters. The task of the early botanist was beset with dangers, hardships and disappointments — rain, starvation, excessive heat, excessive cold, hostile Indians, rats that chewed the hard won specimens, moisture that destroyed them.

For much of our information about the most northerly of our flowers and the extreme northern limitations of the habitat of our common plants we are indebted to J. B. Tyrrel, who, at the beginning of the century went northward by the Mackenzie River and crossed the Barren Lands, returning by way of Chesterfield Inlet and Fort Churchill on Hudson Bay. The dangers along his route were not ferocious Indians and mountain torrents but intense cold, ice, the shortness of the summer and the lack of fuel and food.

These of course, are just the very earliest of the botanists. Within ten years of the publication of Palliser's report, settlers were pouring into the country, the Mounted Police had completed their historic march and the whole aspect of the country had changed. With the increasing population came many botanists, amateur and otherwise, and amongst all the classifying and recording the 'peasant' lore is apt to be lost. It should be dug out now before the last of the old west vanishes.

III. Moon-When-the-Grass-Turns-Green

'Tis sweet, in the green spring
To gaze upon the awakening fields around,
Birds in the thicket sing,
Winds whisper, waters prattle from the ground;
A thousand odours rise,
Breathed up from blossoms of a thousand dyes.
William Cullen Bryant

ON THE EASTERN slopes of the Rockies the winter is long and cold but when spring comes at last, it comes with a rush. Good-Old-Man, the Chinook, comes out of the mountains and rides boisterously over the prairie. All the cold blues of winter turn over-night to brown-pinks and melting purples. Suddenly spring is here and the hills are rippling with glacier lilies, the plains with prairie anemones.

Close against the earth the *Phlox hoodii* lays a carpet of moss and dots it with a host of tiny white and purplish flowers. The low-growing yellow cinquefoil, with its splash of orange in the centre, and its silvery leaves, keeps it company.

The 'sleepy-head' is really not a sleepy head at all but gets up very early and is found with the phlox and cinquefoil.

The 'shooting star' splashes the low-lying meadow with purple and then we know that summer is really on its way. Once started the flowers crowd thick and fast; purple violets, yellow violets, buffalo beans . . . larkspur, yellow bells, pentstemon . . . Before we can catch our breath and count them they are here and gone again to make way for summer's favourites.

PRAIRIE ANEMONE

Anemone patens

A century and a half ago, Alexander Mackenzie stood on the banks of the Peace River holding in his fingers a little purple flower with a furry stem. He described it as a little yellow button with six purple sepals. To him, even then, in spite of its strangeness, it was a sign that his long winter's imprisonment was over and the time for action had come. He prepared his boats and supplies and set off across the mountains for a glimpse of the Pacific and an important place in the history of a continent.

PRAIRIE ANEMONE

Since then this little prairie anemone, that braves the cold winds of spring, has become the symbol of liberty and action, of the freedom of the springtime to many thousands.

According to Greek tradition, Anemos, the wind, employed delicate little flowers as heralds of his coming in the spring. These flowers were listed by Plato as anemones. During the centuries that followed, the name was applied to an entire family of plants with similar characteristics. When, on the western prairies of the North American continent, botanists found plants with all the characteristics of this family they classified them as prairie anemones; literally, flowers of the prairie wind.

In the meantime, however, the flower had become familiar to others less well informed botanically, who had struggled to find for it a name familiar to their experience. People from England, finding that it reminded them of the earliest spring flowers that came up in their lawns at home, called it 'crocus', while from the French and other European travellers came the name of 'pasque flower' from a similiar European species, so named because it bloomed at Easter time and its purple petals were used for dying Easter eggs.

The name of 'gosling' given the downy buds by prairie children is eminently suitable, but the Indian name is even better. The Indians, unhampered by Greek tradition and all the old world sentiment, had a perfect genius for choosing the most poetic and significant name for things about them. 'Ears of the Earth', they called these furry ears which, so soon after the snow drifts melt, the prairie thrusts up to listen for the first faint rustle of summer.

This flower of the springtime, this prairie anemone, has taken such a firm hold on the hearts of the people wherever it is at home, that many stories are certain to grow up around it. The following story explains where it got the fur coat that is such a lovable characteristic. Of course, the scientifically minded will explain that the fur coat is not for warmth but rather for a protection against small pilfering insects, but as flower lovers we are privileged to ignore such rules of cause and effect and enjoy the story for its poetic value.

How the Prairie Anemone Got its Fur Coat

Wapee shivered and drew his robe tighter about him. It was cold there on the hillside, but the shiver was more of fear and loneliness than of cold. Always before he had slept in the tipi of his parents, where his father could protect him.

But at last his father had said, "Wapee is no longer a child. It is time he went to the hills to dream and become a man."

So here he was, by himself, on a hilltop, with great stars above him, the long line of the mountains still sleeping far to the west and nothing about him but a great emptiness.

The morning before he had set out with a light heart. The snows of winter had but lately melted, the sun was warm; and would he not, that very night, dream a great dream that would change him from the child he had always been to the man he was to be? But now the sky was lit by the coming day and all through the night he had lain, not with bright visions, but with dark space and loneliness and fear.

The mountains turned from dark, cold grey to rosy pink, then to purple and last to shining blue, but Wapee still crouched on the hilltop, motionless and brooding. Three more nights like the one just past and he must return to his father and his friends and tell them that he was not a man but only a coward, whom the Great Spirit had found unworthy even of a dream.

The day grew warm and the feeling of great weariness and failure lifted, as it always lifts in the presence of the warm sun god. Besides, Wapee was no longer alone. He had found a friend. Beside him on the hilltop sat a beautiful flower, as white as the snow that was now resting on the slopes of the far-off mountains, before its summer journey to the north land. The flower opened its heart to greet the golden sun and swayed and nodded to Wapee until his troubled mind was calmed by the peace of blue mountains and wind-washed prairie grass.

Wapee sat on the hillside watching occasional crows pass back and forth, or a hawk wheel far above him, or listening to the stir of growing things beneath and thinking grave thoughts. So the day passed.

The mountains turned to rose, then grey. The sun dropped down behind them, leaving to Wapee once more the darkness and the stars, but not emptiness, for now he had a friend, the little white flower, near him.

"Little brother", he said, "It is cold for such fragile loveliness on a night like this. I will lie close and shelter you with my warm robe, but I must not crush you with my big body."

So while one part of his mind slept and rested, the other part kept watch over the flower.

When the dark of the night was just preparing to meet the light of the day, the flower spoke. "Yesterday, Wapee, you were sad because you had been afraid. He who never knows fear is a fool. The wise man learns to overcome it and profits by it."

Wapee sat up with a start and bent over the flower to hear better what it might say but the flower only nodded and swayed in the morning breeze.

All day Wapee pondered on the saying of the flower and next night, when he lay down to sleep, he again sheltered it with his robe of fur. Again, just as Morning Star looked out across the prairie, it spoke.

"You have a kind heart, Wapee. It will lead you to great things."

Next night, still sheltered under the robe, the flower spoke again. "Wisdom and a gentle heart will make of you a great leader. But when you are bowed with troubles and cares, remember that on a nearby hilltop you will find peace and wisdom."

Then Wapee slept and saw, dimly, many visions of what was to come when he should be chief of his tribe and his people happy, contented and prosperous.

Before he rose to go to his people he thought once more of the flower. "Little brother", he said, "three nights you have comforted me in my loneliness and brought me visions. Tell me now three of your wishes that I may ask the Great Spirit to grant them to you."

The flower, nodding, answered. "Pray that I may have the purple blue of the distant mountains in my petals, that men may seek my company and be rested. Second let me have a small golden sun to hold close in my heart, to cheer me on dull days when the sun god is hidden. Last, let me have a warm coat, like your robe of fur, that I may face the cold winds that blow from the melting snow and bring men comfort and the hope of warmer winds to follow."

The Great Spirit was pleased that Wapee's first thought had been for the flower and his prayers were answered. Now over the hillsides thousands of the descendants of Wapee's small white friend face the cold winds of early spring, with the colour of the distant mountains in their petals, a bright sun in their hearts, and a warm furry robe wrapped securely about them.

PRAIRIE PHLOX
Phlox hoodii rich.

One of the earliest of the flowers of the prairie spring grows close to the ground like a spreading moss and is covered with myriads of tiny white or purplish-white flowers. In some districts it is called 'mayflower', in others it is given the delightful name of 'Mother-of-Thousands'. Really a member of the phlox family, the true story behind its scientific name is as melodramatic as any wild west story ever told.

Mr. Robert Hood was an Admiralty midshipman who was appointed to accompany Sir John Franklin on his journey to the Polar Seas. He was to assist in making observations and to make drawings of the land, the Indians and objects of natural history.

They went up the Coppermine River, along the northern shore of the continent. Then in mid-August they began a trek across the Barren Lands, back to their winter quarters at Fort Resolution near the source of the Coppermine, where the Indians were supposed to have laid in a store of provisions.

The French Canadian voyageurs who were employed as labourers were a very irresponsible lot. It was almost impossible to ration the small amount of food available, because, if they were not allowed to eat everything in sight, they not only became sullen, but they stole whatever they could lay hands on. Then, because the canoes were heavy to carry, they purposely fell on them and broke them beyond repair. Their carelessness meant days of starvation and endless trudging around lakes that might have been crossed in a short time by canoe. Facing a cold, sleet-laden wind, walking hour after hour, they had nothing for food except an occasional grouse or a small animal, which they ate flesh, bones and skin, and a sort of fleshy lichen that grew on the rocks.

PHLOX HOODII

"We made a rather sorry meal on country tea and an old pair of leathern trousers", is one entry in the diary of Dr. Richardson, the naturalist. It is quite common to read, "Our breakfast consisted of a small amount of rock tripe and a pair of old shoes."

When they were within a few days march of the outpost of the previous winter, where they expected to find supplies, some of the men became so ill from fatigue, cold, and this diet of soup made from old bits of leather, old bones and lichen scraped from snow covered rocks, that they fell by the way. After several men had died in this way, Hood found that he could go no further and he begged the rest to go on without him. Dr. Richardson offered to stay in camp with the weaker members of the party while the rest pushed on to obtain supplies. Mr. Hood, who was really very ill, Dr. Richardson and Mr. Hepburn were left, while the rest with Sir John Franklin pushed on.

The Franklin party had not gone far when two men became so exhausted that they begged to be allowed to turn back to the fire. Sir John Franklin gave them permission and before long an Iroquois, Michel by name, asked permission also to turn back. Michel is the villain of the story. On his way back to camp he murdered the two voyageurs and stole their guns and ammunition.

All unknowing, those remaining at the fire hailed him as the instrument chosen by the Almighty to preserve their lives, because he brought with him a hare and a partridge which he shot on the way. Michel was a good meat gatherer for several days. He took the axe when he went hunting and he brought in some frozen meat which he said was the meat of a dead wolf he had found killed by the horn of a deer. Not until much later did the rest of the party suspect the true source of the meat they had eaten and learn that it was from the bodies of their dead companions.

As the days went by with no word from the party that had pushed on to the outpost, Michel grew more and more sullen. He refused to hunt, to gather wood, or to help in any way and he threatened to desert them.

Mr. Hood endeavoured to point out to him the necessity and duty of exertion and the cruelty of quitting them without leaving food, but this seemed only to excite his anger. Next day, instead of going out to hunt he remained by the fire to clean his gun and, making it appear to be an accident, he shot Mr. Hood through the head.

After that Michel's actions became so uncertain and so suspicious that it was deemed advisable for the safety of the rest of the party that Michel himself should be put to death and so he was executed by the naturalist, Dr. Richardson.

What has all this to do with a flower?

Through all these hardships, through cold, starvation, through

perilous crossing of rivers and weary miles of trudging over barren
land in the teeth of a blizzard, through illness and heartbreak, Dr.
Richardson clung to his specimens. Amongst them was this little phlox
whose flowers they found from the time they left Fort Carlton, until
they reached the far north. When he returned to England he had the
privilege of giving it its specific name and he named it *Phlox hoodii* in
memory of his less fortunate companion.

CINQUEFOIL

Potentilla pennsylvanica.

There is no glory in star or blossom
Till looked upon by a loving eye.

"No loving eye has fallen upon the modest little five-finger; its
beauty is unpraised", says an eastern author about the eastern cinquefoil. But the modest little five-finger of the prairie finds that
'loving eye' in the heads of small children whose eyes, keener than
those of adults, hunt out the first blossoms of the spring and bring
them in little tight-fisted clusters; cinquefoil, prairie phlox and
dandelions.

They call the flowers of their bouquet buttercups and mayflowers
because, when the country was even newer, no one could answer
their plea for a name except by saying, "They look a little like the
buttercups that used to grow in our pasture" or "They are like the
mayflowers that grew in the woods." Some day a name suited to their
precocious springtime habits will be found and it will be so right that
no one will argue with it.

Before the low-growing cinquefoil has reached the height of its
blooming season, other taller-growing varieties have followed. There
are seventy-nine species of the *potentilla* genus so that during the

summer the traveller in Old Man's country meets them at all altitudes, some modest and retiring, others claiming attention for their size and beauty.

One of the showiest is the tall white cinquefoil (*P. arguta*) which is at home on moist prairies, in thickets and throughout the mountain regions. It and the purple cinquefoil (*P. palustris*) are the only

EARLY CINQUEFOIL

two members of the genus which are not yellow. *Palustris* grows in marshes across the northern part of the prairie region and in the mountains. The flowers, which grow in an open cyme, have small purple petals and a large showy calyx which is lined with deep purple.

All but these two have little yellow flowers like miniature single roses to which family they belong. The leaves are compound, digitate or pinnate and very often, on the prairie especially, they are grey. The divisions of the leaves have given it the name of cinquefoil, a corruption of the French *cinque feuilles* or five leaves.

LONG-PLUMED AVENS

Sieversia triflora

The 'sleepy head' is as truly western as the Jack-in-the-pulpit is eastern. Its queer red stems and buds that never open but hang in groups of three from a central, leafless stalk, were loved as much by the Indian children as by the children of the settlers. They called it 'lies-on-his-belly'.

The purple or long-plumed avens, as it is called in the flower books, is favoured by bees and insects for its sweet nectar. The flower welcomes the bee who pays for his feast by carrying pollen from one flower to another, unless, of course, he becomes too greedy and forces his way in at the side before the flower is open. To protect the flowers from crawling insects that steal the nectar without making any return in pollen carrying, the plant has a hairy flower stalk and drooping flower heads. For the production of nectar in such quantities, water

PURPLE AVENS

is necessary, so the flower is found wherever there is a generous supply of moisture. Far out on the prairie it is found in depressions or buffalo wallows, while near the mountains where the deep snows supply abundant moisture it grows in great red fields.

The colour comes from the dark purple-red of the stems and calyx, the flower itself being creamy white or tinged with pink or purple. The flower never opens out flat like its relative the wild rose, but remains in the form of a tightly closed bell with drooping head.

When the seed is set it ceases to hang its head sleepily. Then the stems turn straight upward and hold aloft heads of long silky reddish hair from which it takes its name of long-plumed avens. The 'sleepy head' of the spring becomes the 'old-man's-whiskers' or 'prairie smoke' of the late summer.

VIOLETS

The pleasure we derive from the violet came across the seas with our ancestors, and even their fondness for it was inherited from long ago. Mohammed loved the violet as he loved no other flower and it is seen often in the designs of the ancients. It was Napoleon's favourite and became the emblem of the Bonapartists, while the deep blue, fragrant English violet has a place no other flower shares in the poetry of the English wayside.

There are many kinds of violets in our country with colours ranging from purple to white and yellow, all of them much loved in spite of the fact that they lack the fragrance of the English variety. The tall white violet with the heart-shaped leaves (*Viola canadensis*) is perhaps the best known of these. It grows up to one foot in height, favouring woodsy locations all across the continent. The upper petals, though white, are violet on the under side, the leaves a rich, dark green. Though blooming early, it lasts well into the summer and has the habit of appearing again in the fall.

The large purple violet (*Viola nephrophylla*), blooming in the spring in moist places, has all the trustful appeal of the true English violet. Of it, as well as of the one he knew, Scott might have said

> The violet in her greenwood bower,
> Where birchen boughs with hazel mingle,
> May boast herself the fairest flower
> In forest glade or copsewood dingle.

There is also a rich purple violet (*Viola pedatifida*) which belongs to the prairie region alone. The leaves of this species are palmately divided which makes it easily distinguishable from other varieties.

The yellow violet is less common as well as less showy. It grows on dry prairies, a small violet that blooms close to the ground, or hides under new leaves along a mountain trail.

Violets, in common with some other plants, have cleistogamic or blind flowers, flowers that never open and lack petals and other advertising agents. These flowers provide abundant seed but are self-fertilized, while the more showy flowers provide for cross fertilization to prevent deterioration of the species. It was on the violet that these blind flowers were first noticed by scientists of the eighteenth century and it seemed such a wonder that they named the particular species the miracle violet.

PURPLE VIOLET and WOOD VIOLET

SHOOTING STAR
Dodecatheon

Some flowers, like the violet, have such an individual and impressive personality that they are taken to the heart of the populace. Violets are

SHOOTING STAR and BIRD'S EYE PRIMROSE

so well known that they are 'violets' in every language — just one universal name for a much loved flower. *Dodecatheon,* on the other hand, with just as powerful a personality, but with less background of lore and legend, has been showered with popular names—shooting star, fish hook and bird bill—all imaginative and showing great interest in its peculiar appearance. Best of all, perhaps, is the name of Indian Chief. The flower is a perfect little prairie Indian with its long nose, the band of vermilion beads about its forehead and the long-plumed head-dress thrown back from its face.

It was discovered in America and introduced into European gardens about 1873, where it was thought of as just another variety of primrose and was called American cowslip. Linnaeus, the eminent Swedish naturalist who is known as the Father of Botany, named it *Dodecatheon* because of a fancied resemblance to twelve gods at the Olympian gathering (*dodeka* — twelve, *theos* — god).

BIRD'S EYE PRIMROSE
Primula farinosa

Of the same family as the shooting star and often found growing in the same moist field is the mealy or bird's eye primrose. It has pink, lavender and occasionally white corolla, flat with a yellow centre. The dark stamens are clustered to form a dark 'pupil', hence the name of bird's eye. The leaves grow in a tuft at the base of the stem and are oblong and tapering with a mealy white appearance. The word '*farinosa*', of course, applies to this characteristic, while the generic name refers to its early season of blooming.

> Primroses, the spring may love them,
> Summer knows but little of them.

BUFFALO BEAN
Thermopsis rhombifolia

The large and important pea family is well represented in Old Man's territory. Many of its members are beautiful and useful plants but two, at least, have an evil reputation. The loco weed and *thermopsis* are violently poisonous.

In spite of this quality, however, the *thermopsis* (called locally buffalo bean or prairie pea) is eagerly welcomed in the spring because of its early and showy blossoms. The stalk emerges from the ground looking fat and downy with a grey coat of silky hairs, its tip curled under and sheltered from the ferocity of the elements. Very soon it straightens into a spike of brilliant yellow pea-shaped flowers from six to fifteen inches high.

THERMOPSIS

One of the most brilliant of early spring flowers, it favours dry open ground, the sunny slopes of the cut-banks for its first appearance and later the open woodlands and flat roadsides.

It is one of the genera found only in the prairie regions.

LARKSPUR

Delphinium

Like the *thermopsis*, the larkspur is a handsome though renegade member of a very well known family, the Crowfoot or Ranunculus, to which belong such flowers as the buttercup, the columbine and even the peony. Unlike the *thermopsis*, however, it is not confined to a single region but belongs to the entire northern hemisphere and has long been a favourite in old world gardens.

According to the Greeks, a fisherman lost his life while saving a

LARKSPUR

dolphin from being captured by some of his comrades. The dolphin carried the body on his back to Neptune and begged that it be restored to life in some manner. Neptune promptly obliged by transforming it into a beautiful flower whose bud was shaped like a dolphin with a load on its back and whose flower had the blue of the seas in its petals. The Greeks called the flower *Delphinion,* which means dolphin. Down through the centuries the name changed very little and when Linnaeus finally got around to making a science of his interest in flowers, by labelling and classifying everything in sight, the name was there for the using. It went into his book as *Delphinium.*

The people of Europe, unacquainted with the Greek story but noting the long spur which is such a characteristic part of the flower, called it larkspur; while the Spaniards, also noting the spur, gave it the name of horseman's spur.

There are several varieties of larkspur which grow abundantly in our territory. The prairie larkspur which is common throughout the prairie regions has deep sky blue flowers and greyish, three to five-parted leaves. A taller, mountain variety, growing from three to six feet high, has a richer, more purple hue and leaves more finely cut.

This plant is the bane of cattlemen who are continually losing stock as a result of its poisonous qualities, but to those interested in it from a less practical point of view its beauty is breath-taking. During early spring it spills cascades of vivid blue down all the coulees of the prairie, retreating gradually as summer approaches, to make its last stand in alpine meadows where it produces masses of bloom of a blue so rich it rivals the shadows of the deep ravines.

FAIRY BELLS AND TWISTED STALK
Disporum trachycarpum and *Streptopus amplexifolius*

One of the pleasures of the springtime is the finding of the dainty bells of the fairy bells and the twisted stalk. Taking shelter from

TWISTED STALK and FAIRY BELLS
Autumn   Spring

the rough winds in clumps of shrubbery, ravines or wooded hillsides, they manage to retain an appealingly fragile look at a time when most flowers have a ragamuffin sturdiness. The leaves are thin and delicate. The tiny creamy bells of the fairy bells hang from the tips of the branches. The twisted stalk strings its bells at intervals up the stalk, hanging them at the axils of the leaves. Twisted stalk, by the way, is a very descriptive name, since the stalk takes a different angle at the intersection of each leaf. *Streptopus* is derived from two Greek words meaning twisted root.

In the rush of early summer flowers these quiet blooms are forgotten until one comes on them suddenly again at the time of the late summer picnic. Fighting to maintain themselves amongst the heavy underwoods they have broadened and coarsened, the disporum especially, producing broad-spreading leaves. The tiny white flowers have become red berries that are a brilliant note of colour amongst the fading greens and yellows of the pre-autumn foliage. Fairy bells produce beautiful, rough, velvety fruit divided roughly into three sections, turning first yellow and then brilliant red and looking very much like a small and brilliantly coloured peach. The twisted stalk has smaller, clear, smooth berries of a darker red which hang like the flowers, at regular intervals along the stalk.

GLACIER LILY
Erythronium grandiflorum

GLACIER LILY

Once upon a time the word violet did not refer to the little purple flower that we think of as a violet. Violets then were sweet scented flowers of many species. It was in those days that a yellow lily with bulb-lets which reminded some obscure botanist of a dog's tooth, was given the name of dog's tooth violet. From Europe the name was carried across the Atlantic and settled on a very similar species, with brown mottled leaves, found in eastern America.

In the western mountains and foothills, from northern Alberta to California, this lily has literally inherited the earth. Here it grows to a greater size and perfection than anywhere else. Its leaves are a pure rich green without the brownish spots.

Early in May, as spring creeps across the prairies and up the mountain slopes, these bright golden lilies clothe the foothills. In such a hurry are they to greet the sunshine that they cannot wait for the snow to disappear but push their spikes up through the snow drifts. As summer advances they follow their beloved snow banks farther into the mountains until, early in July, one meets them far up amongst the snowy peaks where drifts of yellow petals can be seen stretching miles away across the alpine meadows.

The people of the west have discarded the old prosaic name of the eastern species and have chosen in its place the more descriptive one of glacier lily. It has a pure white relative called the avalanche lily, which is also found in the mountains.

YELLOW BELL

Fritillaria pudica

Keeping close company with the glacier lily, rivalling it in the sud-denness of its arrival in the spring and in the bright glossiness of its

FRITILLARIA

yellow petals, and spreading even farther out onto the prairie, is the yellow bell.

The flowers are bright yellow nodding bells which, according to the botanists, are solitary and consist of three petals and three yellow sepals. But the flower itself refuses to grow according to rules. Given the least bit of encouragement in the way of richer soil or a good covering of snow in winter, the stem thickens to support as many as six or eight (quite commonly three or five) nodding bells and the petals and petal-like sepals increase to eight or ten. When the flower opens it is a pale greenish yellow but it turns orange and finally brown with age. Some of its California relatives make no claim to any colour but brown and rejoice in the names of chocolate lily or black lily.

The following quotation from *Steep Trails* by John Muir will strike a familiar note to any who have seen mountain meadows yellow with these two lilies.

> "When the ice of the Glacial Period was laid like a mantle over every mountain and valley — through all these protracted periods, in the throng of these majestic operations, Nature kept her flower children in mind. She considered the lilies and while planting the plains with sage and the hills with cedar, she covered at least one mountain with golden erythroniums and fritillarias as its crowning glory, as if willing to show what she could do in the lily line even here."

GLOBE FLOWER

Trollius albiflorus

A foreground of fat, creamy flowers, just opened beside a brown pool of melted snow; a background of dark pines and snow-covered peaks; and in between these two a group of mule deer go curiously by with ears alert and eyes as brown as the marshy pools; all this greyed and blended in a haze of blobby snowflakes sifting slowly from a heavy sky. This might be the description of a painting by Hiroshige but it is really a scene presented every year when winter and summer meet high up in the mountains.

The globe flower, like the glacier lily, is so impatient to greet the summer that it sends its shoots up even through the snowbanks and is ready to bloom the minute the snow has become brown marsh.

A member of the crowfoot family, it looks like an anemone except for its very large golden centre. The true petals are concealed by the

GLOBE FLOWER

stamens, the sepals being large, petal-like and creamy white. The rich glossy leaves are a perfect setting for the flower head which is set on a stalk about an inch above a bushy circle of leaves.

QUEEN CUP

Clintonia uniflora

A mountain path through heavy woods, especially under firs and spruce, would not be complete without the open faces of the queen cup peering up from the tangled edges. "An exquisite, six-parted flower with heart of gold", says Julia Henshaw. "I feel that a great honour has been bestowed upon me in that I have been permitted to name this lovely plant — queen cup. Hitherto it has been nameless in the English language and it seems to me that no more fitting name could be bestowed upon *Clintonia uniflora.*"

The leaves, from two to five, long, unspotted green, somewhat resembling lily of the valley, make a perfect background for the dainty flower or equally handsome blue berry that follows it. The fruit, though beautiful to look at and conspicuous in all the woods of the mountain slopes, is tasteless and not edible.

The generic name, *Clintonia*, was given first to the eastern species which is yellow with a cluster of flowers, but with the same cool green leaves. It was named by botanist Asa Gray in honour of Dewitt Clinton, Governor of New York state. Thoreau loved the eastern clintonia and felt that it had been misnamed. "Gray should not have named the flower for the Governor of the State of New York," he complains. "What is he to the flower lovers in Massachusetts?" But Gray's sympathisers hastened to point out that Clinton was not only the Governor of New York, but, what was more important, a flower lover and botanist of note.

The western relative of the eastern clintonia has but a single star at the top of a graceful stem and so was called one-flowered or *uniflorus.*

QUEEN CUP

BEAR GRASS
Xerophyllum tenax

Visitors to Waterton Lakes or Glacier Park cannot fail to notice the bear grass which rises like tall lighted candles against the dark evergreens.

Clusters of sharp wiry grass-like leaves grow from a thick root. A woody flower stalk covered with smaller awl-shaped leaves, thin, dry and whitish, rises above this basal cluster and bears a dense raceme of creamy white flowers. The individual flowers are tiny white stars.

The leaves of the bear grass were used by the Indians for making baskets. The blade, which is about two feet long and three-eighths of an inch wide, is smooth and strong and pliant. The young blades particularly, because not exposed to the sun and air, have a smooth, bright appearance and were generally preferred.

As Lewis and Clark returned from their long journey to the Pacific coast, they met the Indians of the mountain regions, laden with neatly packed bundles of bear grass which they were taking to the coast to trade with the coastal Indians for wappatoo roots and for blue beads obtained from the small trading ships that were beginning to find their way up the coast. This bear grass was used by the Indians of the coast in combination with cedar bark for baskets so closely woven that they were watertight, without the aid of gum or resin. The form was generally conic, or rather the segment of a cone, of which the smaller end was the bottom of the basket. They were of all sizes from that of the smallest cup to a capacity of five or six gallons and answered the double purpose of either a covering for the head or a container for water. Some of them were highly ornamented with strands of bear grass, woven into figures of various colours. For the construction of these baskets the bear grass formed an article of considerable traffic.

On the strength of the information collected by Lewis and Clark,

BEAR GRASS

who first called it bear grass, it was given the scientific name of *Xero-phyllum tenax* — the dry leaf that holds fast.

David Douglas, the botanist whose name is familiar to all who have heard of the Douglas fir, sent specimens to England for garden use and one species is named in his honour, *Xerophyllum douglassii*.

Blackfoot visitors to the mountains usually harvested a store of leaves and roots for their own use, and to carry as gifts to their medicinally inclined friends of the prairies who, for one reason or another, were unable to travel so far to replenish their own supplies. They did not need its leaves for baskets, as the buffalo supplied all their requirements along that line, but they boiled the roots and used the resulting infusion for a hair tonic as well as for the easing of sprains. Farther south the infusion was evaporated and the residue used for soap.

Even the ground squirrels find a use for this versatile plant. They cut down the flower stalks and use them for food.

Such a conspicuous plant must naturally have collected many names. A few of the most common are moose grass, pine lily, squaw grass, turkey beard and basket grass.

COLUMBINE
Aquilegia

Until the reign of Charles I early in the seventeenth century, Europe knew only the blue columbine. Tradescant, the King's gardener, so important in botanical history that a whole genus of lily-like plants has been named for him, received as a gift from a kinsman in Virginia a rare new specimen. It was *Aquilegia canadensis,* the gaudy red and yellow columbine of the new world. There was great excitement amongst the herbalists of the day when the plant bloomed.

COLUMBINE

It was rare and lovely — almost invaluable. Gradually, by cross fertilization with the European species, the many garden types of today were developed.

The story of the blue columbine is just the reverse. Carried to New England by immigrants who longed to bring a memory of their home with them to the new world, it escaped from cultivation and made itself so much a home that it is now listed amongst the wild flowers of the eastern United States.

Botanists explain the difference of colour between the European and American species by the efforts of flowers to adapt themselves to visiting insects. Blue, they believe, is the colour beloved of the bees; but in America the humming bird is the guest to be catered to — and humming birds are partial to red.

The western columbine, *Aquilegia formosa*, is very similar to the eastern species except that its spurs are shorter and it is in every way more compact. It is fond of moist, heavy soil and grows abundantly throughout the wooded valleys of prairie and mountains.

A blue flowered species is also found in the mountains but is much rarer than the foregoing.

There is also a variety which is perhaps as well known as any of the flowers of the west since motor trails have been built to the higher lakes. *Aquilegia flavescens* is a graceful, pure yellow species, fond of high altitudes and light, sandy soil.

HAREBELL
Campanula rotundifolia

The bluebell, though connected in our thoughts with Scotland, is equally at home in Asia and in North America. Here it is more commonly known as harebell.

Like the dainty women who came west in covered wagons and faced the trials and hardships with the same courage as the husky men, it is not as fragile as it looks. It is not discouraged by strenuous living but is at home in the most rugged surroundings. Its cool blue sunbonnet is undaunted by the fierce heat of the prairie sun; while its threadlike

HAREBELL

stem bows but does not break before the gales of the most exposed slopes of the upper mountains. Swaying and swinging in the company of the rocks and the skeletons of trees that have given up the struggle with the elements, it sends a soft peal of tiny bells down across the valley.

The scientific name refers to the heart-shaped leaves at the base of the stalk, which wither early, while the stem leaves remain. The thread-like upper leaves and stems reminded the Scotch of hair but the first writers on the subject knew their flowers better than their spelling and their name was accepted by later botanists as it stood.

Other old English names are lady's thimble and witch's thimble.

DANDELION

Taraxacum officinale

Dear common flower that grow'st beside the way
Fringing the dusty road with harmless gold
'Tis the spring's largess which she scatters now
To rich and poor alike with lavish hand
Though most hearts never understand
To take it at God's value, but pass by
The offered wealth with unrewarded eye.

James Russell Lowell

Dan McCowan of Banff tells us that the dandelion was first brought to this continent by the Hudson's Bay Company traders at Fort Churchill, who needed it to balance a diet consisting too largely of meat. Like the English sparrow, it has, by its cheerful, undaunted disposition, made the continent its own. Instead of exclaiming over its unbelievable beauty, as did the king and queen of Siam, when visiting a few years ago, we are apt to pass it by with 'unrewarded eye', taking it as of no more account than the dust by the roadside. And yet there are those who can remember when homesick easterners cultivated a tiny plot of dandelions on the prairies, hemmed in with sunken chicken wire to keep out the gophers and watered with precious water drawn from a well or carried from the river. And children, born in the west, may remember learning these lines from a poem:

Oh dandelion as yellow as gold
What do you do all day?

and having to be told what a dandelion looked like. These people, perhaps, are more apt to take the 'shower of gold' at God's value, though now the hills of the west are, at times, so yellow with the blossoms that they may be seen many miles away.

There is a dandelion which was already on the spot, which did not need to be invited. It is the alpine dandelion (*Taraxacum rupestre*), a tiny slender plant with finely cut leaves and dainty flowers seldom growing more than four or five inches high.

There are also several species of false dandelions (*Agoseris*), plants that look like dandelions but are distinguished chiefly by having smooth seeds rather than the rough ones of the true dandelions. Their beautiful deep oranges and copper colours which at times become almost purplish brown make a beautiful addition to the summer bouquet.

The dandelion, certainly not an uninvited guest to Old Man's territory, ushers in the spring with brave flowers hugging the earth and ushers it out on a deep carpet more golden than the summer sun.

DANDELION

IV. Old Man's Vegetable Garden

If you show a flower to a Sioux, his face will light up, he will smile and tell you its name, its use and, very probably a legend concerning it. The deep resentment which all Indians feel for the white man is due to the wanton waste of the country's natural resources, and the callous indifference towards the land shown by the white settlers. And Sitting Bull said, "I want you to take good care of my land and respect it." It was all too obvious that the white man did not love the country as the Indian understood it.

Stanley Vestal

THE VEGETABLE garden that Old Man planted for his people and set against a background of shifting shadows and purple peaks, would rival any flower garden in its dazzling variety and brilliance. He seems to have taken a special delight in crowning his vegetables with beautiful blooms of every form and colour.

When the garden was all laid out and the flowers blooming, Old Man took the women out across the prairie and through the foothills and showed them which roots were good to eat, telling them at what season to gather them and how to prepare them for eating. This root, he told them, could be gathered in the Moon-when-the-grass-turns-green, but these were not to be gathered until the Moon-when-the-wild-geese-drop-their-feathers. These might be eaten raw, just as they were gathered. Others were to be cooked, or dried, or ground into flour. The seeds of this plant were good for eating and the roots or leaves of that one.

So Old Man instructed his people and they rememberd his lore and kept his garden in the order he had given it to them. Digging around amongst the roots of some favoured patch with a long curved stick known as a root digger, they kept the soil loosened and worked and prevented undesirable plants from intruding, so carrying on a primitive kind of cultivation.

In only two or three cases did they actually plant and cultivate a garden patch. The more southerly of the prairie tribes grew corn, beans and pumpkins in their villages and occasionally a Blackfoot woman would attempt a patch with seeds given her by friends from other tribes. But the tobacco patch was the only garden which concerned the tribe as a whole. In this case an open glade would be chosen where dead wood was burned and the seed sown in the ashes to insure finer plants. Sometimes the seeds were mixed with deer manure in an impressive ceremony, before they were placed in the ground.

CAMAS

Camassia esculenta

When the buffalo were settled on the plains and the sheep and goats in the mountains, when the Indian had learned to hunt for himself and was happy, Old Man gambled with Old-Man-from-the-other-side-of-the-Mountains, whom his people called Coyote Man. Sometimes Old Man won: he won all the buffalo. Sometimes Coyote Man won: he won all the salmon.

It must have been a lucky day for Coyote Man when they played for the camas, that lovely blue lily which early travellers never fail to describe, for Coyote Man has most of it now in his valleys over the mountains. But Old Man has kept a store of it hidden in moist valleys of the foothills. Close to the highway near the entrances to Waterton and Glacier Parks are beautiful blue fields of it.

When it is in bloom no one could fail to notice it or, having once seen it, could ever forget it. Individually, the plants are from one to two feet high, leaves long, narrow and grass-like, flowers rich, purplish-blue borne in a simple raceme. In June great waves of this rich blue sweep northward from California, inundating the land with lakes of blossom.

BLUE CAMAS,
DEATH CAMAS,
ZYGADENE

The large bulb at the base of the stem, somewhat like an onion in appearance, was dug by the Indians soon after the blossoms had fallen. It was baked in a deep hole dug in the earth and lined with grass and heated rocks. The bulbs were laid into the hole in layers separated by layers of grass. Then they were covered with earth and a fire built on top. It required three days and three nights to cook them in this way, but according to the reports of all early travellers it was well worth the effort.

When the pit was opened, a thick, sweet syrup would have gathered on the twigs and strands of grass with which the pot was lined—a temptation to the children and probably to many an adult as well to lick the pot. The cooked bulbs were spread out in the sun to dry and then stored for future use. Occasionally they were pounded, mixed with saskatoons and formed into a sort of cake.

The sticky sweetness explains the name 'camas', which is a Chinook corruption of the Nootka Indian word 'chamas' meaning sweet. The Blackfeet called it Miss-issa.

Busy scenes were enacted in all the camas fields of the mountain regions, where the women dug the roots with pointed sticks and heaped them in great quantities on the plain before packing them in their bags of grass or reeds.

So important a food was the camas in the past that it has found its way into the pages of history books and Government documents; for treaties were made and wars fought over it in the southern States. In geography it also has a place. Villages are named for it in Idaho, Montana, Washington and Utah. In Oregon there is a Camas Valley. The old name for Fort Victoria on Vancouver Island was Camosun or 'place for gathering camas' because of the camas fields with which the city, even today, is surrounded.

In the ceremonies of the prairie Indian tribes the bulb of the camas was often used to symbolize the food given by the Earth Person. For the Sun Dance ceremonies it was cooked with the large leaves of the balsam root and used on the sacred altar.

Amongst the prairie Indians there was a superstition that if the camas bulbs were not properly roasted, if they were under-done or over-done, death would come to the roaster and his relatives. Many families, for that reason, did not care to risk roasting their own, preferring to buy them from the mountain Indians in exchange for the products of the buffalo. Perhaps the superstition arose from the fact that, growing nearby, over the whole of the prairie regions, is a plant that, apart from the bloom, resembles the camas very closely and could easily be mistaken for it once the bloom had fallen. Should one of the bulbs of this plant be included in the baking, death might easily be the result for all who ate of it.

This poisonous plant is known as death camas (*Toxicoscordion gramineum*). The leaves are long and slender, like the camas, and grow in clusters from the bulbs below the surface of the ground. The flower stem grows from the centre of the leaf cluster and bears heads of small, creamy flowers which are quite sweet smelling and attractive. Both the leaf and the root of the plant are deadly poisonous when green. Animals affected by this weed act in a crazed manner which has caused it to be known as crazy weed. It is fairly common in the foothills district and the western range country.

The white camas or showy zygadene is also a closely related species which is exceedingly common from the prairie to the edge of the timber-line. It is a handsome flower which is neither edible, like the camas, nor poisonous like the death camas. It is said, however, to contain some of the poisonous principle but to be seldom eaten by stock. The six-parted, creamy flowers are marked with green at the base and accented with numbers of brown-tipped stamens. They are carried in long loose racemes which sway well above the surrounding growth.

WILD ONION

Allium cernuum

In moist meadows of the foothills, often growing side by side with the camas, is found another handsome lily whose use is obvious to us. Its dense clustered head of rosy-purple flowers tops a long hollow stem which, with the hollow leaves, grows from a generous bulb that has a strong hot flavour. It is *Allium sibiricum*, the purple garlic.

Though a strikingly handsome plant, the garlic is quite over-shadowed from an economic point of view by the smaller variety, *Allium cernuum*, or wild onion. Its grass-like stems and leaves are not hollow and the white or pink flowers are carried in a looser, nodding panicle. It is more common throughout the mountains and reaches farther out onto the dry plains, and the bulb is not as hot as that of the garlic.

Lewis and Clark were very enthusiastic about this small onion which they described as, "growing so closely together as to form a perfect turf, and equal in flavour to the chives of our garden which they resemble in appearance."

Many doubts were current then about the possibility of growing the garden plants of eastern America in the strenuous climate of the west, so one of its recommendations to the minds of the travellers was that "It stands the rigours of the climate well and it will, no doubt, be an acquisition to the settlers."

As a matter of fact, before they got home they found it a decided acquisition to themselves. As they returned up the Columbia before the rush of salmon from the sea, they were reduced to a diet which consisted almost entirely of roots and they used quantities of the onion to correct the ill effects of these roots on their digestions.

Alexander Mackenzie likewise tells of feasting on the small spring onions at almost the other extremity of the mountains, when he was making his famous journey to the Arctic Ocean.

GARLIC and WILD ONION

And half way between these two famous expeditions, Sir James Hector tells of beds of onions where, as he says, the sward seemed to have been ploughed, so torn was it where the bears had been rooting them out like pigs.

ARROWHEAD
Sagittaria latifolia

Often during the war-like history of the western Indians, an ambassador would come from one of the mountain tribes bringing a gift of tobacco to the prairie chief with the offer of peace between the tribes. A long discussion would follow the suggestion and, if the memory of relatives lost in battle was not too fresh and bitter, a truce would be declared. Then the people from the mountains would pay a visit to their new brothers of the plains.

However it might end, the visit always began with much cordiality and the exchange of gifts — trading, we would call it. For the treasures of the prairies, hides, pemmican and other products of the buffalo, the prairie Indians would receive stores of starchy bulbs, especially camas and one called 'wappatoo'. Both of these bulbs grew to some extent on the prairie but not in such large quantities as in the mountains and unless faced with actual starvation, the prairie Indian preferred to hunt the buffalo, like a true aristocrat, and leave the grubbing in the soil to his mountain neighbours.

Wappatoo is one of those bulbs which one finds mentioned again and again in the journals of early travellers to the west. It is at home from the Rio Grande to Hudson Bay and throughout this territory has been the means of saving many a traveller from starvation, though injudicious gorging has also caused many a pain in unaccustomed stomachs. It was the first food sold to Dr. Cheadle's company for worn-out shirts and mangy buffalo hides after their arduous trip down the shores of the Columbia from Jasper House in 1863. Lewis and Clark learned about its value in their westward journey many miles farther south. David Douglas practically existed on it during his weeks of botanizing in Oregon. Paul Kane describes it as similar to the camas but not so dry or delicate in flavour, and also tells us that wappatoo, camas and fern roots are the three main vegetables of the coastal Indians.

This wappatoo of the Indian is none other than our arrowhead, a common plant in our sloughs and backwaters, growing from six inches to two feet in height according to the conditions under which it finds itself. The broad arrow-shaped leaves are, of course, responsible for its scientific name, but these leaves have the unique power of giving

ARROWHEAD

place to long ribbons when the plant is submerged. These ribbon-like leaves allow for a maximum of exposed surface and a minimum of resistance to the current, while the broad leaves ward off too liberal a supply of sunshine. The plant is, therefore, able to adapt itself to springtime freshets and summer drought.

Growing as it does in sloughs and ponds, one naturally wonders how the Indians were able to gather the bulbs from the muddy bottom. The description given by the Lewis and Clark journal is most detailed and interesting.

> "It is collected chiefly by the women who employ for the purpose canoes from ten to fourteen feet in length, about two feet wide and nine inches deep and tapering from the middle where they are about twenty inches wide. They are sufficient to contain a single person and several bushels of roots, yet so light that a woman can carry them with ease; she takes one of these canoes into the pond where the water is as high as the breast and by means of her toes, separates from the root this bulb, which, on being freed from the mud, rises immediately to the surface of the water and is thrown into the canoe. In this manner these patient females remain in the water for several hours, even in the depth of winter."

MARIPOSA LILY

Calochortus

The mariposa or sago lily is one of those many plants that have everything. It is both exquisitely beautiful and of real practical value. Its names are a succession of compliments. *Calochortus* means pretty grass; *elegans,* which is the specific name given to one of our species, means elegant; *mariposa* is Spanish for butterfly and was first applied to the family because of the resemblance of the beautiful Spanish-American varieties to the wings of the butterfly.

Our most common species has three large white petals with a black

spot at the base of each and a generous yellow beard. The petals are
sometimes tinged with purple or yellow-green. They grow in rich open
woods or plains, blooming late in June or July, being especially abundant on the hills and along the edge of the woods in Waterton and
Glacier Parks. In British Columbia and Idaho a similar species is found
blooming across the sage brush plains. Here the Indians call it 'noonas'.

MARIPOSA LILY

The mariposa lily has been chosen the state flower of Utah because
of its service to the early settlers of that country. Between 1853 and
1858, during the famine years, when the country was made destitute
by drought and successive visitations of grasshoppers, thousands of
people subsisted on the generous stores of starch supplied by these
bulbs which were called 'sago' by the Indians who first taught the
newcomers their use.

SPRING BEAUTY

Claytonia lanceolata

Early in the spring when the first purple heads of the prairie anemone are blooming on sun-warmed southern slopes, this fragile little
blossom appears in the muggy wet mould under the willows that still

hold drifts of melting snow. The whole plant consists of two leaves, a slender stem and a cluster of dainty white or pale pink, five-petalled flowers, veined with darker rose. So tender and fragile, the little plant seems more like a shy nymph of the woods, a flake of snow from the retreating drifts nearby come lightly to rest on a stem of green, than a member of a vegetable garden. Yet the Indians boiled and ate the fat little tubers at the base of the stem, that pull up so easily from the sodden soil. They have a nutty flavour, for which reason they are frequently called ground nut, and they contain a good percentage of starch in their composition.

SPRING BEAUTY

It might be well to say that the vegetables used commonly by the Indians of a generation ago are not always agreeable to stomachs accustomed to the over-refined foods of the white man. One of the greatest hardships that early travellers in the country had to face, when their own supplies were exhausted, was the violent illness caused by their first experience of Indian diet. Of course it worked both ways. An oversupply of the food of the white man invariably affected the health of the Indian and for many years the prairie Indians regarded the offerings of the white men with disdain. Only when the buffalo finally disappeared did they make the white man's food their own.

EVENING PRIMROSE
Oenothera biennis

One of the most outstanding beauties of this wild vegetable garden is the evening primrose. Looking ethereal and lovely by the cool light of the moon, but fading rather badly as soon as the hot rays of the morning sun touch her, her great moment comes when most of the other flowers are asleep. The visitors for whom she dresses herself in yellow satin are not the bustling bees of the summer sunshine but grey moths that appear out of the night, sip a moment from her nectar and vanish again into the darkness.

Oenothera is almost entirely an American species. Only one species, a native of Tasmania, is indigenous outside of the North and South American continents, though several have been introduced into Europe. On the grassy prairies and arid regions of the west there are a great many varieties, mostly with large yellow or white flowers.

As indicated by its name the plant is a biennial, that is, it lives two years, putting up a rosette of green leaves the first year and blooming the second.

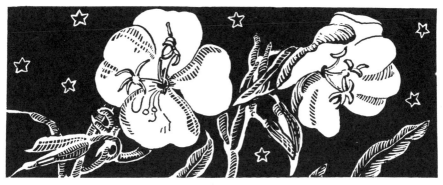

EVENING PRIMROSE

The large four-petalled flower advertises a nutricious, stocky root which the Indians gathered in the autumn and dried for winter use. It is a close relative of the primrose which Europeans have introduced into their gardens because of its large edible root which they cook or serve in salad.

The farmer classes them as weeds and so we see, by a queer twist of fate, a man digging out and casting aside a vegetable which has for centuries helped to feed the Indian race, and replacing it with a vegetable which has for centuries helped to feed the European race

VETCHES

According to 'A Survey of Canadian Plants in Relation to Their Environment', published by the the Department of Agriculture of the Dominion of Canada, there are forty-nine varieties of *astragalus* and twenty-four of *oxytropus* in Canada without even mentioning all the other divisions of the pea family. Of these many are beautiful, brilliantly-coloured flowers that paint the prairie and mountain slopes in various shades of cream, purple, magenta and blue, causing Palliser to exclaim when he first saw them, "The prairie is magnificent, *astragali* especially forming a great ornament to it." John Macoun, also, when he paused west of Qu'Appelle in 1879 could not resist making an entry in his diary about them. "Flowers are a most conspicuous feature of the prairie. *Hedysarum* and the various *Astragali* vieing with the lily and the vetch in loveliness and luxuriance. Often, whole acres would be red and purple with beautiful flowers and the air laden with perfume."

Of the many vetches that cover the prairie, several have proven themselves useful for vegetables. The Indian milk vetch (*Astragalus aboriginorum*) is perhaps the least prepossessing of all the vetches as far as appearance goes. It is a long scrawny plant with whitish leaves and loose racemes of tiny flowers of a dirty white tinged with mauve.

Its calyx, seen through the lens, reveals stiff, blackish hairs. In bloom one would scarcely notice it unless purposely looking for it, but in seed it is more conspicuous, bearing long, semi-elliptical reddish pods. It grows in open meadows and along the edges of the cut-banks. It has

INDIAN MILK VETCH

acquired its name from the fact that the plains Indians gathered its slender yellow roots to add to their vegetable diet.

The Canadian milk vetch (*Astragalus canadensis*) is a much more handsome plant. It has fifteen to twenty hairy leaflets and long dense spikes of yellowish-white flowers with, occasionally, a blue-tipped keel. The Blackfeet called it 'tender root' and ate it either raw or boiled.

LIQUORICE

Glycyrrhiza lepidota

Alexander Mackenzie had become well acquainted with liquorice root long before he came across it on the upper beaches of the Mackenzie River. He was able to add one more root to the diet of the natives, for they were ignorant of its qualities as a food and had considered it a weed of no value. Though Mackenzie and his men, who had plenty of meat in their diet, found its astringent qualities too active and had to discontinue its use after several days, it seemed to form the proper balance for the diet of fish, roots and berries on which Lewis and Clark and their men were existing.

LIQUORICE

The Indians along the Missouri and Columbia Rivers, however, knew it well and sold generous supplies of it to the Lewis and Clark party. The roots were roasted in embers and then pounded lightly with a stick, in order to separate the strong ligament in the centre of the root, which was then thrown away. According to their report it then had an agreeable flavour not unlike that of a sweet potato.

The plant is a common one on the sandy beaches of the prairie rivers and along the roadsides wherever there is sufficient moisture. It has all the appearance of being the common weed that the Indians of the Mackenzie River considered it. The leaves are pinnate, with eleven to nineteen blunt-tipped leaflets. The flowers are yellowish-white, pea-shaped blooms about half an inch long. The seed pods are like a reddish-brown burr appearing on the plant while the leaves are still fresh and green, making it more striking in seed than in flower. Perhaps these burrs, which are troublesome in the wool of sheep, are responsible for its being listed as a weed.

PRAIRIE POTATO
Psoralea esculenta

"The feast to which the Indians invited us consisted of cooked dog, pemetigon and a kind of ground potato, dressed like the preparation of corn called hominy, to which it is little inferior. It was placed before us in platters with horn spoons. We took pemetigon and potato."

This was on the westward journey of the Lewis and Clark expedition, when they were camped in Montana. Had it been the following year, when their journey across the mountains lay behind them, they would almost certainly have accepted the cooked dog in preference to the potato, for hunger can overcome many of the polite shrinkings of the educated palate. This, however, was their first introduction to cooked dog as a part of the menu. It was also the first time they had met that most famous of all prairie roots — the prairie potato.

Enjoyment of this root as food seems to have depended entirely on the conditions under which it was served. Captain Palliser, meeting it first at Red River when his own stock of provisions was still intact, condemns it as insipid, unnutricious trash.

It was, however, such a staple article of food among the Indians and half-breeds of the country that it received such names as prairie turnip, prairie potato, and Indian bread root, *pomme blanche* and *pomme de prairie*. Many of the trappers and traders, as well as the Indians, depended on it for life when game was unobtainable.

What a relief it must have been to many a houskeeper in a prairie schooner, when supplies were running short, to have a pedlar in blanket and moccasins appear at her nomadic doorway with sacks of these edible roots. No wonder that they bought them eagerly and laughingly called them by the name of the staple which was lacking—bread, potato or turnip. The *voyageurs*, having long before learned its use under similar trying circumstances, had made it a regular part of their diet. It seems strange that this root, that was the mainstay of the Indian tribes for so many generations and that played its part so valiantly in the building of the west, has now passed out of the common experience of the people of the country and has, so soon, become almost a nameless weed.

These tuberous roots, one and a half to two inches long, resembling a dahlia tuber, contain a large percentage of starch and sugar. They were dug late in the summer and were eaten raw, boiled, roasted or dried in the sun and ground between stones for flour to mix with soups and stews.

In appearance the plant somewhat resembles the lupine and was at one time classed as one, being called *Lupinus tuberosa*. It has blue, clover-like flowers, like the lupine, but the spikes are shorter and more densely crowded. The five leaflets are smooth above and hairy beneath. Both leaves and stems are covered with black scurfy dots, which were responsible for taking them from the company of the lupines and giving them a name of their own. *'Psoralea'* means rough or scurfy.

SILVERWEED

Potentilla anserina

"One of our loveliest and most odious weeds, with a cheerful and active disposition, whose slender runners, which root and form new plants like the strawberry, have carried it around the globe." So C. F.

Saunders describes the silverweed in his book on California wild flowers. He tells of Reginald Ferrer who was presented in Tibet with bowls of silverweed tubers, little nutty things like young asparagus or new potatoes. "It seems strange", he continues, "that the California aborigines, with their flair for detecting economic worth in the wild plants, should not have learned of the silverweed's edible roots." The Blackfeet, however, called it 'dry root' and used it roasted in the same manner as their other roots.

SILVERWEED

This is one of the weeds that the white man hoed out with merciless determination when he planted potatoes in the first garden patches of the west. It was ignorance that made him thus destroy the Indian's food; and it was through ignorance that the Indian achieved his revenge. It was during the famine years and the lean years that followed that potatoes were planted for the first time in many parts of the new country. Wondering, the Indian watched the white man putting valuable food into the ground instead of taking it out; tubers that the Indian knew would make several meals for his hungry family. So, at night, he crept to the potato patch and dug up all the potatoes that the white man had planted during the day. For a few days at least, the Indian's family had enough to eat and the new country was in danger of going down in history as a place where potatoes would not even come up.

PRAIRIE TURNIP
Lithospermum linearifolium

Out on the dry prairie a little yellow flower grows in flat-topped leafy clusters. Its yellow, salverform, five-cleft flowers hold a tiny drop of nectar in the rounded base of the tube. Children of the prairie love to steal the nectar, sipping it from the bottom of the tube and then, perhaps, swallowing the whole flower. It is a deep tap-rooted perennial, the leaves of which are linear, covered with short stiff hairs.

To botanists it is known as *Lithospermum linearifolium* or puccoon. The French called it *Plante aux Perles* because of the hard, stony seeds that mature in the calyx, at first soft green, later hard, white and shining. The early flowers, which appear late in May, are clear bright yellow; but later ones, faded by the sun's hot rays, are inconspicuous and pale.

The sweet nectar-filled tops, which the children of the prairie so soon discovered, were not overlooked by the original inhabitants, for they were dried by the Indians and used for incense.

The long roots are edible and nutritious. According to one writer they are shaped like a carrot and taste like a turnip, for which reason the plant was called, by the traders, wild turnip or prairie turnip, though Palliser says that "it assimilates to that plant only in growing underground, being more the shape of a carrot or Jerusalem artichoke and by no means of the most tender nature." Its degree of tenderness, however, mattered little to those who knew how to use it, for the Indians pounded it fine and dried it in the sun, forming a sort of flour which when boiled in fat broth was "one of their most dainty foods".

The Blackfeet called it Pono-kau-sinni or elk-food. Another Indian name was Mas-etomo. Early writers often refer to it as 'mas' or 'mats'. It was the only vegetable the present Indians of one western reserve could remember when asked about the food of their grandparents.

BALSAM ROOT
Balsamorrhiza sagittata

French explorers along the St. Lawrence River in the seventeenth century found the Indians preparing and eating tubers which reminded them of the artichokes to which they were accustomed at home. Gathering some of the seeds, they sent them back to France where they immediately caught the popular fancy and were served on many a table under the name of *Pommes de Canada*. In Italy they were called *Girosole Articcio* — from girosole (literally turns-with-the-sun), the Italian name for the sunflower. Thus they gradually became known as sunflower artichoke or Jerusalem artichoke, Jerusalem being a corruption of girosole.

When trappers and traders who were familiar with this artichoke in its native haunts, found the Indians of the foothills digging the roots of a yellow sunflower-like plant, it seemed quite obvious that it was just another artichoke. In their amateur flower lists it became known as western artichoke, though the true sunflower artichoke does not venture west of the Mississippi Valley. By botanists it has been given the descriptive name of *Balsamorrhiza sagittata* — *sagittata* meaning arrow-leaved and *balsamorrhiza* meaning balsam root.

As a food it was used in many ways. The fresh tender leaves of early spring made a juicy salad; the seeds were ground into flour known in the southern idiom as 'pinole' and made into a sort of biscuit. In these districts, where it furnished food for early settlers, it was known as mormon biscuit. The tender portion of the root was also used as an addition to the stew of the Indian population. It is surrounded by a resinous rind so potent as to remind one of all the evil-smelling cough mixtures of turpentine, balsam, white pine and tar that crop up with the annual round of winter colds, but when this dark rind is peeled off the white centre proves quite mealy and edible.

Captain Lewis describes an incident on his westward journey, just as they approached the mountains, which throws an interesting light on the labour-saving devices employed by the Indian women who did not have spades for digging these roots from the tough prairie sod but had to depend on a pointed stick.

> "When we stopped for dinner the squaw (wife of the half-breed guide) went out and, after penetrating with a sharp stick, the holes of the mice, near some driftwood, brought us a quantity of wild artichokes, which the mice collect and hoard in large numbers."

During the month of June and early July, the open slopes above the camas and garlic fields are terraced with bright yellow blooms like 'little sons of the sun'. The flowers are very like sunflowers in appear-

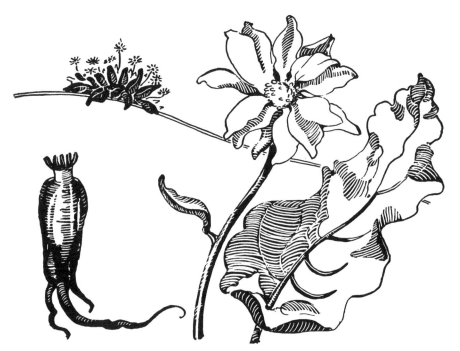

BALSAM ROOT

ance with long yellow rays and yellow centres. But it is the leaves that form the characteristic feature of the balsam root. Even after the flowers have disappeared, the plant may be recognized by the clumps of large, arrow-shaped, greyish leaves from which it takes part of its name. These leaves were used by the Blackfeet in their Sun Dance ceremony, being cooked with the sacred camas bulbs which symbolized the purifying of the body from within.

BRACKEN

Ferns, which from medieval times have been used for the concocting of spells and witchery, which symbolized to the superstitious mind all that savoured of black magic, may well have had much the same signif-

BRACKEN

icance for the sun-loving prairie Indians, for whom the dark forest aisles and gloomy valleys held ghosts and evil spirits. Trips to the mountains for lodge poles, for hunting of game and gathering of roots were frequent. Wars were fought on forest trails and parties travelled far inward to the country of the Kootenai and even, occasionally, as far as the 'Stinking Water' itself; but men never went into the woods alone and women only entered them in pole gathering parties which were under the protection of the men. Their home was in the sunny woodland and on the prairies.

Here, along the edge of the forest, far from its gloomy depths, they found a fern to contribute to their larder. In open woods and sunny meadows grows the commonest of all ferns, the bracken. It is a coarse plant with much divided leaves which grows under favourable conditions to a height of six or eight feet, though the average height is about three feet. It can easily be distinguished from other ferns by the fact that the fronds grow singly rather than in the usual ferny clusters.

Both the stem and root are edible, that part of the stem which is between the curled up tip and the hairy base being used when the frond is still fresh and tender. It is very moist and juicy when eaten raw and provides a substitute for a drink when water is not easily obtainable, or it may be boiled and treated like asparagus.

The roots, also, were eaten by the Indians who seemed to enjoy a bitter, astringent quality in foods which the white man finds unpalatable. These roots are covered with a thin black bark which is brittle and tough but easily separated from the edible part. This inner part, after the root is roasted, resembles the dough of wheat both in appearance and flavour.

So commonly were these roots used by the coastal Indians that Paul Kane lists them with the camas and wappatoo as the main vegetables of the Indians whom he was visiting.

SUNFLOWER

The sunflower, like the sparrow, seems to belong about buildings. Perhaps it is because the sunflower has been domesticated for so many, many years.

In the days when long lines of Indians in paint and feather might be seen riding across the prairie to the great Sun Dance festival, followed by long rows of squaws and travois-laden horses—or even before that when the travois were drawn by dogs and women, when there were yet no horses—the sunflower was domesticated in many parts of the world.

But here in the west, where it was at home, those were the days of the sunflower's majesty. Then it was really a plant to be treasured for its worth. The small oily seeds were gathered and the oil removed by boiling. This oil was used for food or for oiling the body and hair—a primitive beauty treatment. The seeds were also ground into a nutritious flour and made into great flat cakes. Their use is described in the journals of Lewis and Clark who exclaim again and again of the beauty of the sunflowers through which they were travelling.

SUNFLOWER

"Along the bottoms we observe the sunflowers blooming in great abundance. The Indians of the Missouri and more especially those who do not cultivate maize, make great use of the seeds of this plant both for bread and for thickening their soups. They first parch them and then pound them between two stones until they are reduced to a fine meal. Sometimes they add a portion of water and drink it thus diluted; at other times they add a sufficient proportion of marrow grease to reduce it to the consistency of common dough and eat it in this manner. The last composition we preferred to all the rest."

In Mexico and the Great Lakes district the sunflower was cultivated, but here on the edge of the mountains and out on the great plains, it went its carefree way providing food for the tribes unhampered by fence or hoe.

Spaniards found it in the south, in the early sixteenth century, and sent it home to Spain where it caused a flurry amongst the gardeners of the day. In Russia it received special attention and was cultivated and bred until the great Russian sunflower was evolved, with large edible seeds which in this country are fed to poultry but in Russia are roasted and eaten like nuts.

The little black seeds of the prairie variety are smaller, but exceedingly nutritious and so, in the days that are past, it was an important and useful member of plant society. Now it has become a tramp and has taken to the road where it sits, a little roadside philosopher, nodding and smiling in spite of adversity, rejoicing in the heavens and the sun which are the property of all alike.

DOCKS

The members of the dock family are as handsome as they are unusual. Perhaps if they were less common, their appearance would receive more attention, but anything listed in the weed book, as four of its members are, is apt to have its beauty slighted.

Docks are, usually, coarse plants with thick roots. The flower has no petals, but a six-parted calyx, the three inner divisions of which develop into wings on which the three-sided seed is carried by the wind.

In California, C. F. Saunders tells us, the dock *Rumex hymeno-sepallous* is used for rhubarb in the pies of the desert housewife. The tuberous roots contain a permanent dye used by the Navajo to stain wool yellow and are so rich in tannin that the Mexican population used them for tanning hides.

DOCK

Farther north, the Blackfeet discovered these same properties in a related species, *Rumex mexicanus*, which is abundant in the foothills and mountains. They called it yellow root and used it for a dye, as well as for a medicine for the healing of many ailments. A large, coarse plant, growing several feet high, it has long bluish-green leaves and pale yellow flowers. The fruit is dark red and the stem is strongly grooved. It has not found its way into the weed book as yet, nor has *Rumex venosus*, its striking cousin of the prairies.

Rumex venosus is one of the numerous species which are confined to the prairie regions of this continent. It does not grow very high, seldom reaching as much as two feet, but it makes up in beauty what it lacks in size. The large three-winged seeds grow in dense panicles, the wing-like sepals being green at first but turning to a bright pink in age.

It is easy to guess why it has been given the popular name of wild begonia. That is the first name that would suggest itself to anyone who knows that popular house plant; for *Rumex venosus* looks very much like a favourite begonia that has been petted and fed until its blossoms have reached unusual size and brilliance. The reason for the name of 'sour greens' is also obvious, since the tender shoots of so many of its relatives were used to replace rhubarb and spinach in the kitchens of the pioneers.

It has received its specific name of *venosus* because of the veined or venose appearance of its large seeds. It was named by Frederick Pursh, very likely from a dried specimen gathered by Lewis and Clark in 1806 and was never actually seen by him in its native habitat. This is probably the reason for the veined appearance, rather than some other characteristic, receiving so much emphasis.

It is fond of a sandy soil and it seems to have found plenty to its liking in Alberta, Montana and Saskatchewan. In fact it seems to be fast qualifying for that place in the weed book which, so far, it has managed to avoid.

The weed book relatives of these docks are the curled dock, clustered dock and bitter dock, as well as the sheep sorrel.

MOUNTAIN SORREL

Oxyria digyna

One of the delights that European hay fields hold for children is the sheep sorrel or cock sorrel with its acid flavoured, edible leaves which they love to chew. This sorrel, which is really a dock, *Rumex acetosella*, has been introduced into our country and is now a common weed in all parts of the continent.

A closely related species which is indigenous to the mountain areas, is the mountain sorrel. It is abundant at high altitudes, in moist meadows above the timber-line, and, lower down, along lake shores and streams. J. B. Tyrrel found it also far to the northward, especially at Chesterfield Inlet and Ashe Inlet on Hudson Bay.

The plants have thick, fleshy tap roots. Rounded, kidney-shaped leaves are clustered at the base of the stem which bears the usual panicles of red and green perianths. It is a showy and conspicuous flower which one never fails to meet on summer hikes through the mountains.

The leaves have the same pleasantly acid flavour of so many of the docks and are recommended for use in the same manner as cress, as a filling for sandwiches or as a garnish for salads.

The Indians of the mountains, so Alexander Mackenzie discovered, used it as a principal food and article of commerce with the Indians of the coast. The women boiled it with berries and salmon roe, in large wooden kettles. When it reached a certain consistency they took it out with ladles and poured it into frames of about twelve inches square and one inch deep. It was then exposed to the sun until it became

MOUNTAIN SORREL and ALPINE BISTORT

dried into cakes. These cakes were prepared in large quantities for food and as an article of traffic.

POLYGONUM

Growing beside the sorrel in alpine meadows or on mountain rock-slides is another member of the buckwheat family which proved of value to the Indian cook. Growing from eight inches to two feet in height, the heart-leaved, or common bistort, *Polygonum bistortoides*, has narrow, somewhat heart-shaped leaves with rolled back margins. The flowers are mostly white with red stamens and pink bracts that give a pinkish look to the whole. The stems are solitary or clustered with racemes of closely packed blossoms. It is not the leaves that are used as is the case with other members of the family, but the thick, oblong rootstock. The Indian cook added them to the soups and stews which formed the main dish of every Indian meal.

The serpent grass or alpine bistort, *bistorta viviparum* is a smaller relative of the common bistort. It is a dainty little flower which is extremely common in moist spots of the mountains and was one of the first flowers to attract the attention of Captain Palliser as he began to note the change of vegetation between prairie and mountain regions. The flowers are greenish, white or pink, growing in dense, narrow spikes. The seeds are dark brown and dull. The flower spikes are viviparous, that is, in place of the lower flowers, a small bulblet or plant develops and strikes root when it falls to the ground. This type of reproduction frequently occurs amongst plants in the arctic regions. The alpine bistort is also found in meadows along the edge of the Barren Lands.

COMMON NETTLE
Urtica lyallii

Emerson's definition of a weed is—a flower whose virtues have not yet been discovered. If the compilers of weed books guided their selections by this definition, surely the common nettle would not be found so often in the company of weeds.

It is, of course, most famous for the fine stinging hairs with which the plant is covered, but as a vegetable it needs no introduction either in Europe or amongst the pioneers of the new country. Its use as a green was as common as the use of pig-weed, dandelion and dock and much more common than spinach in the days when spinach was an imported vegetable and nettles grew abundantly along every stream and in every hollow. In the seventeenth century nettle porridge was a common dish in England and a good cook was said to have been able to make seven different dishes out of nettle tops.

The Indians of the northern lakes and rivers, who depended on fish for their living, made use of the fibres furnished by nettle stems for another unique purpose. With them they made a fine rope which they used for their fishing lines and nets. The first traders who came to the country preferred these native-made nets to the hempen nets that they brought with them from 'Canada', declaring that they were finer, smoother and not so quickly affected by the water.

Several species of nettle are used by modern manufacturers for the making of cordage, paper, thread and grass cloth.

PARSLEY'S WESTERN RELATIVES

Set in deep valleys under the grass-covered slopes of the foothills, run little clear-eyed brooks almost hidden beneath overhanging willows. The banks are covered waist deep with many-coloured flowers, wild geraniums, purple fleabanes, pink roses, yellow gaillardia and many others. Woven, like a lacy web, through all the tangle of coarser bloom are the dainty flowers and slender, fern-like foliage of the western members of the parsley family. In the shadow of dark coniferous forests and on the dry hillsides of the prairie, they are equally at home.

An old English proverb tells us that the parsley seed goes to the devil and back nine times before it comes up, not because it is at home in such company, but because it was such a favourite in old English gardens that the gardeners of the day got impatient waiting for the slow germinating seeds to sprout. Actually the parsley is a very respectable individual, the head of a large and respected family which includes the parsnip, carrot, celery, dill and anise.

In ancient Greece its fragrant leaves and blossoms shared with the laurel the distinction of adorning the victorious brow of Hercules. It was also used in wreaths for festive occasions and funerals.

The far western members upheld the family tradition for usefulness. Old Man taught his people to use the roots and stalks of the various parsleys for food and the leaves were given a place in the ceremonials, both festive and solemn, of the Indians of the plains and mountains, though they could have known nothing of its honourable position amongst the ancients.

COW PARSNIP

Heracleum lanatum

In early spring the Indians must have looked forward as we do to the first fresh rhubarb. In official circles their rhubarb is known as cow parsnip. The first tender shoots of the spring were gathered and roasted over coals or cooked in much the same manner as our own rhubarb. Early settlers learning this, gave it the local name of wild rhubarb.

Alexander Mackenzie describes it as a very 'grateful' vegetable, for he and his *voyageurs* gathered the tops and boiled them with their pemmican. The borders of lakes and rivers along which they passed on their way to the Pacific Ocean in 1792 were covered with its luxuriant foliage. He tells us that it was a favourite food of the Indians whom he encountered. They roasted the tops over a fire and then, taking off the outer rind, had a very palatable food.

Growing at times to a height of eight feet, it has spreading leaves, and its tiny white florets are carried in umbels which often measure a foot across. It is a lover of damp soil and is found on moist hillsides, in swampy hollows or along the edge of the woods.

In his interesting account of the Sun Dance of the Blackfeet, Walter McClintock describes its use as a symbol in the very important ceremony of raising the centre pole, around which the Medicine Lodge is constructed. The altar for the Sun Dance was made by cutting away

COW PARSNIP

short prairie grass and smoothing the soft earth. It was lined with juniper. At the foot, bending towards the west, was a single stalk of wild rhubarb with an eagle plume fastened to the top of it. These were used as symbols of lightness and were believed to favour the safe raising of the centre pole. If the pole fell or any mishap occurred, disaster was believed to follow. Because of its use in these ceremonies it is sometimes called 'sacred rhubarb'.

ANGELICA
Leptotaenia multifida

Another member of this useful family is the cut-leafed angelica—the 'big turnip' of the Blackfeet.

It grows on the grassy slopes of the mountains where it flowers in June. The plant is from one to three feet high. The blossom is brownish purple, carried in umbels of three to four inches in diameter, the finely cut leaves forming a leafy base from a fleshy rootstock. It is a most striking plant. The seeds are flat and slightly concave and are provided with lateral wings which are broad, very thick and corky.

This plant found a place very early in Blackfoot mythology, as we are told in one legend of the beaver bundle. When the chief of the Beavers came ashore to present the Beaver Bundle and all the details for the celebration of the Beaver Ceremonial to the Blackfoot chief who had set up his lodge on the banks of the Kis-is-ska-tche-wan or Swift Flowing River, he entered the tipi and handed the red-painted willow tongs and a sack of incense to the chief. The incense was the dried leaves of the angelica.

With sacred willow tongs, the Blackfoot chief would lift a coal from the fire to the altar. Then, laying on it a piece of the incense, he would purify himself in the smoke so that he might listen to the sacred things that the Beaver chief had to tell him.

As well as having a symbolic use as incense, this handsome plant was also used as a food and a tonic and was mixed with the brains of the buffalo and used for tanning hides.

The highly scented stems, after being dried, were cut into small pieces by the mountain Indians and worn in strings about their necks.

TWO OTHER PARSLEYS

Two other parsleys are worthy of mention here for the service they rendered to man before the roads were opened that brought food from the markets of the world.

Atenia Gairdneri with its dainty white flower heads and slender many-parted foliage, growing three to four feet in height, is like a refined cow parsnip. Its slender finger-like tubers, from one to four of which are attached to a single stem, were used raw or boiled, or added as flour to the inevitable Indian stew. When fresh the root is white, firm and crisp and when dried and pounded it makes a fine white meal. It was one of the roots most easily digested by the white man and was used by Indian mothers to feed their children.

The Snake Indians called it yampah. To the Shoshones it was known as yearhah, while the Blackfoot name for it was nits-ik-opa, double root or squaw root.

In coniferous forests grows a shadow-loving parsley which looks much like the squaw root. It has the same dainty flat-topped clusters and finely dissected foliage, in place of the broad, heavy leaves with which the parsnip shelters the soil and retains moisture for itself. This is the western sweet cicely (*Osmorrhiza obtusa*), which depends on the trees to preserve its moisture and reserves its energies for attracting insects. The white bloom is like a beacon in the dark forest and as an added attraction it provides a sweet scent. Even the thick, edible roots are scented and attract ground animals and rabbits as well as men.

Lewis and Clark describe a busy scene which must have been typical

of many an Indian encampment where these roots were gathered. The mill which ground them to flour consisted of two stones in the busy hands of a woman. They tell us that the noise made by the women pounding the roots sounded something like a nail factory!

BISCUIT ROOT
Cogswellia

"We still place our chief reliance on the mush made of roots (amongst these the Cows and Quamash are the principle) with which we use a small onion which grows in great abundance, and which corrects any bad effects they may have on our stomach. One of our men to-day brought home three bushels of roots and some bread of Cows which in one situation, was as important as the return of an East Indian ship.

The bakery from which these precious supplies were obtained was an Indian camp where the women had worked industriously, digging the roots from the nearby flats and grinding them into flour. The medium of exchange was white and blue beads.

The 'cows' of Lewis, written variously 'cous' and 'cowas', was another of the famous roots of the early west, which belonged to the parsley family. This root is the well known *racine blanche* of the French Canadians and the biscuit root of the American and British settlers that followed them. On occasions these roots were eaten raw, when they had a taste somewhat resembling raw celery; but usually they were ground into a fine white flour and made into bread which was in the form of large flat cakes.

Cogswellia is a low-growing parsley, apparently stemless. The little, flat yellow and occasionally white umbels, growing close against the ground, surrounded by its circlet of fern-like foliage, resembles a little old-fashioned corsage. Out on the prairie it shares with the cinque-foil and the white prairie phlox the honours of the earliest springtime.

Strange that such a respectable and helpful family should contain a criminal strain. Yet one of the best known poison plants of the world is a member, so closely resembling the edible varieties that it is a simple matter for the less observant to make a mistake. The spotted cowbane is believed to have provided the poisonous potion which ended the life of Socrates.

It grows throughout our territory in swampy places and is listed in the weed books as dangerous to cattle. Both stem and leaves

COGSWELLIA

are poisonous to some extent but it is generally the lower leaves and roots that prove fatal to livestock. In spring these roots are more poison-ous than at any other season. Then it was gathered by the Indians for arrow heads destined to be used in warfare.

There are several species of poison hemlock, all very similar to the edible members of the family. For this reason travellers usually left the gathering of cous to the Indians, it being safer to risk hunger than immediate death by poisoning. To the French *voyageurs* this plant was known as *Carrot à Moreau*.

Shortly after the half-breeds of the Palliser expedition found that they had a botanist in their midst, a group of them came to Monsieur

Bourgeau and requested him to take notice of a mysterious noise issuing from the swamp. This noise, they told him, came from a certain plant which possessed a very powerful 'manitou'. It not only had the power of poisoning, but it continuously kept up a muttering noise which invariably became silent at the approach of men.

Determined not to let doubt stand in the way of so important an addition to botanical knowledge as a sinister plant with a voice under its own control, Monsieur Bourgeau, accompanied by Sir James Hector, set off into the darkness (*moreau*) of the swamp with a lantern.

Stepping carefully, they crept up to place after place from which the sound proceeded, but always, at their approach, the muttering stopped. At last they effected a stealthy approach and quickly turned their light in the direction of the muttering, now almost at their feet. This time success met their efforts. They interrupted a noisy little frog in the midst of its croaking.

CAT-TAIL

Almost everyone is familiar with this striking inhabitant of the damp, rich marshlands or wayside sloughs. The name *Typha latifolia* is descriptive, '*typha*' meaning a bog and '*latifolia*' meaning broad leaved. The cat-tail, though found throughout the mountains, does not like too high altitudes.

So decorative is it that it has been used in design and painting the world over. Perhaps its best known role is that of mock sceptre in the hand of the Master in many of the paintings of the crowning of Christ with thorns, by early Italian painters.

The flower head is monoecious, the staminate heads occurring higher up on the stem than the pistillate. The fruit is supplied with hairs attached to the flower stalk to allow of dispersal by the wind, but the plant does not depend entirely on this method of reproduction. It has a creeping root-stalk, fibrous roots and erect stems. The main stalk branches through the mud and sends up new leafy stems every spring. Finally it decays and all the new stems become plants in their turn. In this way a single plant may populate an entire marsh in a very short time.

It is these creeping root stalks that bring the plant into a chapter on vegetables. They contain a core of almost solid starch, containing the same amount of protein as rice and corn but less fat. Although they have a somewhat insipid flavour, they were dug and dried by the Indians and ground into flour, or were served roasted or raw.

On the Pacific coast where they were plentiful, the broad leaves from which the plant receives its name were commonly used for the weaving of mats and platters. When an important guest arrived, clean rush mats were spread and fish, berries and roots placed before him on platters made of rushes. The dead were often buried in canoes wrapped in large mats of rushes and tied securely with cords made of the bark of the cedar.

CAT-TAIL

WILD RICE

The wild rice, a tall grass bearing long black grains, grows about the edges of the lakes in the area just west of the Great Lakes. It was of great interest to early travellers who were so dependent on the strange new country for food. The Indians had long known about this useful plant and Daniel Harmon describes their method of garnering it.

> "It is gathered about the end of September. The natives pass among it in canoes. Each canoe has in it two persons, one of whom is in each end, with a long hooked stick in one hand and a straight one in the other. With the hooked stick he brings the heads of the grain over the canoe and holds it there while with the other he beats it out. When the canoe is thus sufficiently loaded, it is taken to the shore and emptied there. This grain is gathered in such quantities, in this region, that in ordinary seasons the N.W. Company purchases annually, from 1200 to 1500 bushels of it from the natives, and it constitutes a principal article of food at posts in the vicinity."

After the rice was gathered it was usually dried first in the sun and finished in a pot over the fire. The separation of the grain from the chaff was done by 'treading' it in a hide spread in a shallow pit. New moccasins or bare feet were recommended. It was winnowed by being deftly shaken about in a shallow birch bark tray when the wind would help to spill the chaff over the edge. The clean grains were stored in bags of rushes.

All expeditions into the west stocked up on this basic food before leaving Lake Winnipeg. Away up on the Peace River, Alexander Mackenzie mentions using it as food for his men who came in from a difficult excursion frozen and almost at the end of their strength from starvation.

The French Canadian *voyageurs* had a name for the rice — *folle avoine;* and the Indians called it menomin, from which one tribe took the name of Menominee.

It grows in water about two feet deep where there is a rich muddy bottom. It rises more than eight feet above the water and its appearance bears a considerable resemblance to oats. It belongs to the same family as the rice of commerce and there were various ways of preparing it. Parched, as a porridge, ground into flour, or made into soup with the fruits of the district, it had a high food value.

Today this Canada or Indian rice is the favourite food of ducks, geese and other wild fowl. It is marketed to a limited extent as there is a demand for it as a game food, but it is difficult to harvest because the seeds ripen unevenly and drop as soon as they mature.

LABRADOR TEA

Ledum Groenlandica

Perhaps it is because the Englishman loves his tea and many of the early writers were Englishmen, that the Labrador tea holds such a prominent place in the literature of the newest world. But think what a cup of hot tea would mean after a day's trek over snow and ice in temperatures far below zero and with an empty stomach.

Franklin says, "Not being able to find any *tripe de roche*, we drank

LABRADOR TEA

an infusion of Labrador tea and ate a few morsels of burnt leather for supper."

How much more depressing would be the effect if that passage had read "melted snow and burnt leather".

If the Barren Lands should ever require a national flower emblem I hasten to suggest the Labrador tea. The food failed, the nourishing root crop failed, the rock tripe failed, but the low evergreen shrub of the Labrador tea was always there to supply a comforting infusion.

> "Since our departure from Point Lake we had boiled the Indian tea plant, *Ledum palustre,* which produced a beverage in smell much resembling rhubarb, notwithstanding which we found it refreshing and were gratified to see this plant flourishing abundantly on the sea shore, though dwarfish in growth."

Point Lake is on the Coppermine River above the 29th parallel, the sea referred to is the Arctic at the mouth of the Coppermine.

Ledum groenlandica, the Labrador tea so abundant in moist sections of our territory, varies slightly from that of the far north but still has the characteristic foliage — oblong, with margins that curl under, green and slightly wrinkled on top with rust coloured wool underneath. When in flower the plant is beautiful enough to have been introduced into old country gardens as an ornamental shrub. Each individual blossom consists of five white petals with a large green ovary in the centre, the style and numerous long stamens adding to the decorative effect of the flower clusters.

Ledum is a member of the heath family and is related to the heather and the rhododendron.

MUSTARD

To serve with all this staple food a condiment is required and we find this in the mustard family. It needs no introduction. Indeed, who could serve a meal without it? Perhaps no other family except the roses, the peas and the grasses is so useful to us. To this great family belong the crisp, biting herbs, radish, horse radish, and mustard cress. Cabbage, cauliflower and turnip are also of this group.

Mustard itself has long been used in medicine and as a condiment; but it was not until the eighteenth century that the idea of grinding the seeds to a powder and mixing them with water was first conceived. The inventor of this new palate tickler was an English woman. Her preparation was tremblingly submitted to that lover of good things, George I. His majesty tasted and approved.

For this purpose the black mustard seed is best, but it is rare and expensive so seeds of the white mustard are usually mixed with it. In Palestine black mustard attains a great height — up to twelve feet — and is probably the one referred to in the New Testament parable of the mustard seed which became a great tree. *Brassica nigra* is listed as a weed but it has not become a menace.

Our first thoughts of mustard are as weeds. Tumbling mustard, ball mustard, hare's ear mustard, pepper grass, shepherd's purse — all the vast array of yellow and white four-petalled flowers that crowd our waste places may be met in the weed books. But there is one redeeming feature of this family's character. Out of 1800 species not a single unwholesome plant is found.

The decorative members of the family found in our territory are the rock cresses, low-growing plants similiar to the sweet alyssum and arabis of our gardens. The white, pink or purple flowers are easily recognised because of the four-petalled Greek cross of the *Cruciferae* family.

BITTERROOT

Lewisia rediviva

Among the dried specimens which Captains Lewis and Clark picked up on their famous journey to the Pacific and sent to the botanist Pursh, was a dry mass which seemed to Pursh to contain a hint of life. He planted it and it grew. To come to life again after several years as a dried specimen seemed such a remarkable achievement that Pursh named the plant *Lewisia* after its first collector, and *rediviva* for its manner of resurrection.

Sir William Hooker, director of the Royal Botanical Gardens at Kew, had an even more remarkable experience a half century later. He immersed the plant in boiling water to kill it for herbarium use. A year

BITTERROOT

and a half later, noting that it still did not seem quite dead, he planted it and it produced a perfect plant with handsome flowers.

So much for its scientific name and nature, which seem, for once, to match each other beyond argument. Having no European counterpart and being so unique that botanists placed it first in the cactus family but finally settled it into the family of the Portulaca, the common name was left to the invention of the pioneers. They settled unanimously on a characteristic of its root and named it bitterroot. The Indian name of spatlum with which it was labelled is said by one writer to be a mistake since 'spatlum' means tobacco. Another writer says it is known locally as tobacco root because of its tobacco-like odour while cooking.

However this may be, it is the nutritive quality of the roots that originally made the plant famous. It has been placed second in importance amongst the food plants of the dry belt west of the Rockies, being preceded by camas and followed by *Balsamorrhiza, Lilium colum-biana, Erythronium grandiflorum* and *Fritillaria lanceolata.*

It is described as a slender root, an inch or two long, as thick as a goose quill and white like short lengths of spaghetti. When dried and scraped these roots dissolve in water like pure starch. But what a tremendous task to gather enough to feed a family!

The bitterroot was important enough in its day to have given its name to a mountain range, a river and the Bitterroot Valley which lies between the Rockies and the Bitterroot Mountains. Its habitat is not confined strictly to the valley of its name but extends northward into British Columbia and southward to Yellowstone Park and California. It also penetrates into one corner of southern Alberta.

So closely is it related to the history of Montana and so firmly did it establish itself in the hearts of the settlers of this country of great ranches, boom towns and mines, that in 1895 it was made the Montana state flower.

V. Old Man's Medicine Bag

I have been acquainted with fifteen different tribes of Indians. The tribes that are most enlightened and that have advanced the farthest towards civilization are the Sauteux and the Crees. These tribes have a greater knowledge than other Indians, of the medicinal qualities of the bark of trees and of herbs, roots, etc. and their medical skill enables them to tax heavily other tribes. Indeed their medicines, with their skill in regard to their application, form considerable articles of commerce with their neighbours.

Daniel Harmon

MANY AN Indian woman had her bag of 'simples' gathered from the flowers around her, for the curing of minor complaints or for use on the patient before the weird incantations of the Medicine Men were called upon as a last resort. That the healing powers of some of them should be purely imaginary and mixed with superstition is not surprising when we remember that not so long ago, in England, the medicine cabinet held a file of many recipes which called for grass grown in a churchyard, leaves picked by the light of a full moon, or roots dug by the seventh son of a seventh son. So in the Indian camp many remedies, popular a few years ago, have gone rather out of fashion now. There are many of them, however, that may be found on the shelves of the modern dispensary, and many of the plants of the country have been found to contain valuable elements that the Indians did not suspect.

To the mediaeval European as well as to the Indian of half a century ago, the lichen that hangs in long hairs from the pine trees, and goes by the name of old man's beard, was a popular hair tonic. In common with all primitive people they believed that the appearance of the plant had much to do with its curative powers.

The plants of the country and bits of lore picked up here and there, were often a help to the early traders and settlers who were called upon to supply medicines for every sort of ailment. One day a superstitious hunter might ask for a medicine to chase away the Evil Spirit who followed him into the woods and blew at the game from behind his shoulder, warning it of his presence. The next day the trader might be called upon to treat a foot half severed by the blow of an axe, or a poor body tormented with ulcers. Whatever the ailment, a treatment must be found or the trader would lose the confidence of his men.

Mackenzie tells of treating the hand of one of his men to which the thumb was hanging by a thread of flesh. The natives had been treating it by dancing round the patient and blowing on the wounded part. He applied a poultice of bark stripped from the roots of the 'spruce fir', after having first washed the wound in the juice of the bark. This was a very painful dressing but in a few days the wound was clean. He then applied a salve made from Canadian balsam, wax and tallow dropped from a burning candle into water. With this preparation he dressed the wound three times a day during the course of a month and found that it healed nicely.

All the amateur cures practised in the days when doctors were scarce, however, did not turn out so successfully and many amusing stories are told by old timers of the painful results of some of their experiments.

CLEMATIS

Judged by the well-worn theory that like cures like, the best hair tonic of the foothill country, and one moreover that was actually used for that purpose, is the lovely clematis. In August it piles up mounds of silken grey-white hair among the trees and up the banks, as if some thrifty housekeeper were gathering mounds of freshly carded wool for autumn comforters, or Storm Bringer were laying by his supply of winter snows.

There are two species of clematis indigenous to this part of the country. One is *Clematis ligusticifolia,* a rather temperamental vine which grows so abundantly in some sections of the country that not only the trees of the river bottoms are bowered in white but all the banks, the railroad tracks and even the prairie itself are wrapped in its woolly blanket. In other districts quite nearby it is entirely absent.

Not only in autumn is the name of 'traveller's joy' an appropriate one. Early in spring its grey woody branches bud into tender green com-

CLEMATIS

pound leaves that twine around each nearby twig until the whole shrub is wreathed and arches swung from tree to tree. Then the whole plant breaks forth into strands of creamy stars that dip and sway to every passing breeze as if the tree were strung with fairy lanterns.

A daintier vine with smaller, more pointed leaves is *Clematis columbiana*. It loves the woods and mountain slopes where its flowers, consisting of inconspicuous petals and four or five big blue sepals, look like lovely blue butterflies hovering amongst the greenery. One approaches them warily lest they should suddenly take wing. This clematis is most conspicuous in June when the flowers are in bloom, for though its seeds are strung with silvery hairs it does not form into the great downy mounds of the *ligusticifolia*.

The twining leaves (it has no runners) which bend to clasp each twig or stalk that comes within its reach, carry the weak rope-like stem here and there, not far above the forest floor, where it forms a network that seizes the ankles of the unwary traveller, tripping him with invisible strands like ropes strung by mischievous boys on Hallowe'en. As a result it has earned from the Indians a name very different from the traveller's joy of its white relative. They called it ghost's lariat.

WOOD ANEMONE

Anemone Globosa

Closely akin to the clematis, though none but a botanist would suspect it, is the western anemone, another member of the crowfoot family. Its five-petalled, white, pink or red flowers and many-parted foliage are a familiar sight in the springtime woodlands and even out on the prairie wherever a bit of moisture gives it encouragement. It is a hardy plant that stands the coldest of winds and roughest of weather without complaint. Its little dark seeds are wrapped in great puffs of batting, which burst from the thimble-like heads in the late summer when the whole plant has ripened, making it almost as handsome in seed as it is in bloom.

Because of these soft puffs of wool the Indians called the plant 'looks - like - a - plume'. They burned the cotton batting seed-wrapping on coals to give them relief from headaches.

On the slopes of the mountains, usually growing in thick woods, is a somewhat similar anemone (*Anemone parviflora*) which has a dainty solitary flower with a bluish tinge at the base. Both these anemones are sojourners in northern latitudes as well and have been found far north of Lake Athabasca and along the shores of Hudson Bay.

WOOD ANEMONE

AVENS

Sieversia triflora

As a hair tonic, the long-plumed avens whose hairy seed heads cover the summer slopes of the foothills with reddish mists, should have proven quite as popular as the clematis, though for some reason difficult to explain, it seems not to have been put to that use. It was, however, used as a wash for sore eyes of which the glaring sun and smoke-filled tipis must have caused a goodly number.

The long-plumed avens is a curious little red-bracted plant with heads carried in triplets, the flowers of which never seem to open. It has been mentioned before under the name of sleepy head and prairie smoke.

A relative of the long-plumed avens is more widely known for its medicinal contents. It is found from Newfoundland to British Columbia, in swamps and on low grounds or in thickets. A tall coarse plant, twelve to twenty-four inches tall, it has strongly toothed pinnate leaves. Its five-petalled flowers are pink with deep purple veins and a purplish calyx. Its popular name is water avens; its scientific one is *Geum rivale*.

The Spanish called it *Herba Benedicta* and used the thick, fragrant, reddish-brown, creeping root-stalk for the making of ale and wine. In some parts of the country the peasants made a drink of it that was dark in colour and was served with milk and sugar. Its tonic, astringent qualities also made it a popular remedy for tuberculosis.

WATER AVENS

FIRE WEED

Epilobium angustifolium

The fire weed, that tall spike of magenta blossoms, which from July onwards is seen everywhere along the roadside and through the aspen

FIRE WEED

thickets, carries in its veins an antiseptic which was used by the Indians for the healing of sores and ulcers.

But its greatest use is for the healing of burns, the burns of the earth itself. Wherever a fire has swept across the mountain-sides the fire weed creeps in and hides the charred stumps, wrapping a brilliant pink bandage over the blackened bones of the forest. It makes way for the quick-growing aspens that follow on its heels and in their turn provide shelter for the slower-growing evergreens which will, in the course of a century or so, replace the forest that disappeared in a day.

One legend of the fire weed tells of an Indian maiden. To rescue her lover from an enemy tribe which was preparing to torture him, she set fire to the forest about their camp. While they fled before the flames she lifted the wounded man and carried him off through the woods. Some of the tribe, unfortunately, saw what she was doing and followed her. With her heavy burden she could not travel fast enough to escape but wherever she touched her moccasined feet to the black ashes of the forest floor a flame sprang up in her wake and drove the enemy backward. When at last they gave up the chase, flames still continued to leap about her but they took the form of a brilliant flower that blazed through the blackened skeleton of the forest long after she had passed.

Another common name for the fire weed is willow herb. This plant forms sheets of colour through the gigantic scenery of the Jasper Highway — acres of gravel bars of the wide river beds are covered with its flowers. It spreads across the prairie too wherever the soil is to its liking, favourite locations for it there being the slopes of railway embankments, fence corners and partly cleared woodlands. Across the northern areas of the provinces it grows as it does nowhere else. It is impossible to think of the Peace River country without being reminded of the fire weed. Even John Macoun who crossed the continent in flower time was impressed. Of Hudson's Hope he says:

> "Clumps of willows and poplars of various ages were interspersed with the most astonishing growth of herbaceous plants I ever witnessed. Willow herb and a number of other tall-growing species covered the whole region with a thick mass of vegetation that averaged from three to five feet in height."

There are other species of the willow herb found growing throughout the region; a water willow herb which grows in wet places and marshes; an alpine variety, lower growing, bearing fewer but much larger flowers; and also a white species with red-tinged seed pods.

BANEBERRY

Actea rubra and *Actea alba*

Without the low-growing mats of baneberry, the woods of the foot-hills and mountains would lose much of their springtime charm and their autumn splendour. The foliage itself, which is deeply cut and

BANEBERRY

coarsely veined, is handsome enough to make the plant outstanding in a world of handsome plants. But in spring it raises snowy panicles of bloom that love to silhouette their freshness against the dark trunks of old pines or the black rotting mould of last year's leaves. By August the white panicles are replaced by spikes of berries of a startling shiny redness or a white so pure and opaque that, on their account, the plant has been called china berries or doll's eyes. These brilliant berries with their polished surfaces are one of the chief glories of the autumn woods.

The berries are mildly poisonous, and on this account they have become known as baneberry, though they are not so poisonous as to prevent the robins from stealing a favourite cluster.

The roots of both the red and white species were boiled by the Indians and used to cure the colds of the prairie long before the white man came with his remedies in bottles.

The plant makes a handsome addition to the garden and is easily grown. Though it takes the seeds two years to germinate and the plant several more years to come into bloom, they are easily moved and once established are very long lived, blooming and bearing their fruit year after year.

MINT

Mint was one of the earliest of plants to attract man with its healing powers, along the Mediterranean as well as in North America. The very smell of it is soothing and healing and naturally draws attention to itself. During past years it has attracted to itself such names as self-heal, heal-all, motherwort, pennyroyal, tea-vine, horehound and prunella. The Indian, who has a flair for suggesting the most significant aspect of a plant in its name, has called it quick-smell.

Wherever the extract of a plant is prescribed as a cure for nerves or mental disorders, as so many of the mints are prescribed, one feels that the directions on the bottle should read, "Three doses to be taken daily on the spot where the plant grows." For if a cupful of mint tea or a spoonful of mint jelly is a tonic for frayed nerves, how much more powerful its curative properties would be if mixed with a skyful of sunshine and floating clouds and a breezeful of woodsy scents.

Europeans used their mints for sore throats and gargles. The Spanish Californians called it *Herba Buena* and made of it a wholesome drink. The prairie Indians used it also for tea and medicine and conceived the delightful idea of lining their parflêche bags with its leaves before filling them with the dried meats they were storing for winter use. Used in this way it must have provided the same complement to their meals as mint jellies and sauces do to our mutton roasts.

BERGAMOT

Monarda menthaefolia

The most handsome of all the mints of the west is the bergamot. It is little thought of in the eastern part of the continent where the flowers of the large heads open only a few at a time, giving a ragged appearance to the whole plant. But in the heat of the prairie sun the western species opens all of its flowers

MINT

at once, covering the heads in a dense mass of purple bloom.

John Macoun has left a description which gives us a glimpse of the prairie when it was very new to the white man. He tells us of his first meeting with a band of Indians shortly after he left Fort Garry on his first trip to the west in 1872.

> "A handsome brave came first with a painted tin horse hanging down from his neck to his naked bronze breast, skunk fur around his ankles, hawk's feathers on his head, and a great bunch of sweet-smelling mint (Monarda) on one arm to set him off the more. They were dressed just as I had read in books, with breech cloths around their loins and a few bead ornaments about their bodies and all the rest the colour of bronze on account of the sun shining broadly on their naked bodies."

BERGAMOT

How easily the sturdy flower fits into the picture! Many plants have received the name of 'old man' because of their long white hair, but the Blackfeet have given this flower, with its clean vigorous habits, the very appropriate name of 'young man'.

In the country along the shores of the Columbia River where the natives existed almost entirely on a diet of roots, Lewis and Clark found many of them afflicted with a strange disease which caused them to lose completely the use of their muscles, though the rest of their faculties seemed unimpaired. When some of their own men began to be affected in a similar manner, they resolved to try the remedy suggested by one of the members of the party. Building a sweat lodge after the fashion of the one so much in favour with the Indians, they placed the patient in it. During the sweat bath he drank copiously of a strong infusion of horse-mint (*Monarda*) which was used as a substitute for seneca root. This treatment proved to be very effective and the patient soon returned to normal life.

DOGBANE

Apocynum

Throughout the west, especially in the mountain districts, the spreading dogbane is a common plant. Its branches are widely forking and bear thick, light green leaves, slightly hairy beneath, which make a lovely contrast to the small, pale pink, bell-shaped flowers with turned-back lobes.

The names of some of our plants which are listed in old botanies are based on quaint superstitions that have, in many cases, been forgotten. So it is with the dogbane. Just why and when it was poisonous to dogs no one seems to know but that is what the name '*Apocynum*' means — a plant that dogs should keep away from.

It would, perhaps, have been more to the point if it had been called flybane. Its innocent looking little pink bells have a fiendish habit of catching small flies whose tongues are not long enough to reach in to the hidden nectar nor strong enough to loosen themselves after making the attempt, so that they are kept suspended by the tongue until they die.

There is, however, an element of poison running through the

plant and when a branch is plucked it exudes a milky juice strong enough to blister a tender skin. This juice was used by the prairie Indians for cleaning buckskin, and contains a percentage of rubber high enough that an attempt has been made to use it commercially. The root is very bitter and has been used to replace ipecac as an emetic.

The flat seeds of the dogbane are provided with a long silky coma or tuft of hairs at the end, on which the ripened seed floats down the wind. This silken hairy attachment probably suggested to the Blackfeet that the juice would be a good hair tonic. Most of the men of the prairie

DOGBANE

tribes took great pride in their long glossy hair, combing and oiling it and encouraging it to grow longer and shinier in every way possible. But there was a belief amongst them that too large a dose of this natural hair tonic would turn the hair grey, and they called the plant 'makes-your-hair-grey'. Perhaps some ambitious brave, thinking that since a little juice of the dogbane was good for the hair, more would be better, applied too liberal a dose and found that his hair had been whitened or his scalp blistered.

ALPINE SPEEDWELL
Veronica

Speedwells have been looked upon as flowers of good fortune. To present a parting guest with a sprig was to ensure him safety and success in his travels.

The Latin name is traced to a pretty legend. When Jesus, the cross on His shoulder, was approaching the place of crucifixion, a maiden pitied his sufferings and gave him her handkerchief. The Saviour wiped the sweat and blood from his face with it; and lo, a perfect impression of his countenance appeared on the cloth. Ever since this true likeness (*vera iconica*) has been preserved at St. Peter's and is revered as having marvellous healing powers. The maid was canonized as St. Veronica. Some of the speedwells were formerly valued as remedies—hence the application of the name to them. The Dutch call it 'honour and praise' because of these medicinal qualities.

Blue flowers are usually linked in our thoughts with some high virtue. With speedwell we overlook the coarse or insignificant leaves of the various species and think only of the flowers that have a touch of the blue of the skies of the mountain meadow—and we give to this flower a meaning closely akin to that of the forget-me-not which it somewhat resembles.

SPEEDWELL

PRAIRIE STICKING PLASTER
Grindelia

In August the prairie puts on its most dazzling robe, all embroidered with yellow flowers. There are sun-flowers, arnica, ragworts, dandelions, golden asters, goldenrod and, most ubiquitous of all, the gum weed. It is forever underfoot, clutching at your ankles with sticky fingers as you cross a vacant lot, or poking its round face in at the back gate to gaze at the more favoured flowers of the garden. If it were possible to mistake the flat yellow flower heads, one touch of the bracts beneath would identify it, for in them is secreted the resinous substance that gives the plant its character. Its use to the plant is somewhat of a puzzle to botanists, who suggest that it may serve the plant as a protection against parasitic diseases or undesirable insects.

Larger resinous plants like the pines use their gum to fill up wounds made in their trunks. From them the Indians learned to use the gummy substance to heal their own cuts and wounds. Out on the prairie far away from the pines, the sticky heads of the *grindelia* were used, the

GRINDELIA

gummy surface being placed over the wound like sticking plaster.

The leaves and early blooms were steeped to make a beverage prized for its tonic qualities. It was used to purify the blood and to clear up colds and lung trouble.

Grindelia is one of those ancient prairie remedies which have found their way into the respectable society of modern medicine.

BLADDERPOD
Physaria didymocarpa

The bladderpod is a handsome member of the mustard family that looks as though it had escaped from someone's rock garden. It is a low little plant, growing no more than a few inches high, with a central rosette of sinuately-toothed leaves. Outside the leaves, forming a com-

BLADDERPOD

plete yellow circle around them, the bright yellow, four-petalled flowers are clustered in June. By July the flowers are replaced by fat inflated pods that grow close together in pairs like little Siamese twins. The plant usually grows on dry cut-banks or along the gravelly margins of streams. The roots which support this quaint little plant are tap roots that travel on and on into the ground in search of water. You may dig up as much as four feet of root and still find no lessening in the thickness, no sign that the end of the root is near.

The scientific name was chosen because of the inflated seed pods, *physaria* being the Greek word for bag or bellows. The Indians chose the equally suitable name of 'grey leaves' for it.

The whole plant seems ideally suited for decorative work both in the garden and in designs but the Indians found a more practical use for it in curing sore throats.

YARROW
Achillea

There is not a meadow nor a pasture, scarcely a back yard anywhere even in the heart of the city, where a plant of yarrow might not be found. So common is it that we walk over it scarcely realizing that it is a flower.

The yarrow or milfoil has a story that reaches back to the beginning

YARROW

of history. Its scientific name is *Achillea,* given it in honour of Achilles, who made an ointment from it to heal the wounds of his soldiers after the battle of Troy. According to legend, Achilles first learned its use from Chiron the centaur. All through the Middle Ages it was stored in monasteries, in convents, in apothecaries' shops and in household medicine chests, to be forced down the throats of anyone who, in a moment of weakness, admitted to an illness. The whole plant was dried and brewed into a tea which was administered as a cure for a run-down condition or for indigestion.

Because of its finely cut fern-like leaves it was known as milfoil or millefolium, the plant with a thousand leaves.

There are several species found on the prairie and in the mountains, but all seem so similar to the casual observer that the differences are of little interest.

WILD SARSAPARILLA
Aralia nudicaulis

Sarsaparilla

The wild sarsaparilla is a flower which impresses us by early blooming in June and its choice of a beautiful location under the tender green of poplar woodlands, rather than by any special charm of leaf or flower. The somewhat woody stem is extremely short. From it rises a single long-stalked compound leaf and a naked flower stalk bearing usually three umbels of numerous little greenish, five-petalled flowers sometimes tinged with pink. The purplish-black fruit ripens late in the season to complement the yellow leaves.

It is, however, by reason of its root-stalk that it is famous. This is very long, sometimes nearly three feet, and aromatic. While the true sarsaparilla of medicine comes from a South American plant, this plant furnishes a commercial substitute used as a blood purifier and a summer drink.

It is a close relative of the ginseng so well known to the wholesale drug business in eastern America.

ST. JOHN'S-WORT

Hypericum scouleri

Along the banks of snow-fed streams high up near the timber-line, one comes upon mats of little yellow flowers clustered at the tops of leafy stems. The leaves are in pairs along the stalks. The flower has five yellow petals and numerous long stamens that give a feathery appearance to the cluster. The buds are brilliantly tipped with red. It is called St. John's-wort and is a far western relative of a plant famous in the household medical circles of a day not so long gone by.

The European variety is fast becoming a weed of American roadsides. Out of Asia it came, marching westward across Europe and from there to America.

Gathered upon Friday at the hour of Jupiter, it was hung in the windows of European peasants' homes on St. John's Eve to drive away the evil spirits who delight to roam abroad on the eve of a saint's anniversary. Carried about in the hand it would drive away spirits or reveal the presence of a witch. The Italians called it 'devil chaser'. Young girls planted it and if it grew, the coming year would make them brides. Hung over the doorway it would protect the house from thunder and lightning. But these were by no means all the wonderful properties it contained. It had another name — 'balm of the warrior's wound'. Soaked in oil, it was a cure for wounds from poisonous weapons. Taken internally it was a cure for melancholia.

In spite of all these powers there seems to be no mention made of its use amongst the Indians.

RAGWORT

Another plant famous in the annals of mediaeval flower lore in Europe, but equally at home in this western hemisphere, is the ragwort or St. James'-wort. All the wonders of the St. John's-wort were repeated by the St. James'-wort on the eve of St. James' Day, July 25th. It was also used for healing wounds.

From early spring until the autumn snows creep down the mountain, the ragworts cover the rocks and woodlands with their bright golden heads. Their yellow petals out-shine the blue

SAINT JOHN'S-WORT

richness of larkspur and the flaming paint brush of early June and mingle still with the purple asters in autumn. They bloom in the valleys of the foothills and on the prairie roadsides and they lift bright faces to greet the climber on the windswept shale far above the timberline. Of all the western flowers they are the most perfect artists at choosing a location and background, clinging to the corner of a precipice where they look down into gloomy valleys, silhouetting themselves against a dark, spray-moistened rock, leaning far out over a white waterfall or standing high against the transparent darkness of a mountain lake.

They have yellow daisy-like heads, usually growing in clusters and shading from pale yellow to rich saffron and orange. Their scientific name *Senecio* refers to their hoary-headed seeds and comes from the word 'senex' meaning old man.

P. A. Rydberg, in his *Flora of the Rocky Mountains and Adjacent Plains*, lists 114 varieties of ragworts in Old Man's territory. Strangely enough, with all these varieties running loose over the country, the only one to find a place in the weed book is an immigrant from Europe. And, as so often happens, this handsome and respectable family bows under the name and reputation of the one black sheep.

That the plant has the strong juices that originally put it into the category of medicinal plants is proven by the fact that in Antigonish

YELLOW RAGWORT

county, in Nova Scotia, it was discovered that this imported weed caused a curious and fatal disease of the liver in cattle. This disease, previously supposed to be contagious, is now attributed to quantities of the weed in hay.

WOOD BETONY

WOOD BETONY

Pedicularis bracteosa

Worn about the neck and cultivated in grave yards as a charm against evil spirits, the betony was believed to cure every ill that man falls heir to. In fact, the doctor to the Emperor Augustus counted forty-seven diseases for which it was a specific. When the Italians wish to praise a person they say he has more virtues than betony.

But beauty is not one of its virtues. It is a tall coarse plant with heavy fern-like foliage. On top of reddish stems grow large hairy spikes with small greenish-yellow or dull red flowers, which resemble a parrot's beak with raised, hooded upper lips and small lower ones.

The genus *Pedicularis* and its allies are known as semi-parasites. They possess chlorophyll and so are able to manufacture some organic substance out of inorganic materials, but they supplement this food source by attaching themselves to the roots of other plants.

Sir William Hooker tells us that the common name of this plant is a corruption of *'bentonic'*, from *ben* or head and *ton,* good or tonic. Our wood betony is, of course, merely a new world edition of the plant that gathered this old world lore about its head. The European variety is called *Bentonic officinalis.*

BROOK LOBELIA

BROOK LOBELIA
Lobelia kalmii

The slender brook lobelia sways softly among the tall grasses at the edge of a stream or stands half immersed in a sun-warmed swamp looking up with innocent blue face, all unconscious of the evil reputation of its tropical and even some of its American relatives. Many of them contain a milky sap in which a narcotic poison occurs. Some varieties were highly thought of as a drug.

Erasmus Darwin describes a venomous West Indian species:

And fell Lobelia's suffocating
      breath
Loads the dark pinion of the gale
   with death.

Lobelia was named by Linnaeus in honour of de L'Obel, an old botanist of Flanders who became physician to James I of England.

Perhaps *Lobelia kalmii* should be allowed to redeem its family's reputation, and should be listed as a healer since, in these days, its beauty and its choice of surroundings count for much.

FLAX

Linum lewisii

One of the sights which caused Lewis and Clark to write in glowing terms of the new country they were passing through was the fields of blue flax which they noticed day after day as they drew nearer and nearer to the mountains. They had perhaps seen specimens of the blue flax of the old country which had furnished the fibre for linen materials and the oils for medicines. But in the eastern part of the continent even the cultivated variety was so rare in those days that one writer on wild flowers wonders if Longfellow ever actually had seen a blossom when he wrote, "Blue were her eyes as the fairy flax."

Now Lewis and Clark, as they passed through Montana, saw it all day along the river banks and picked it wherever they stopped.

> "For several days we have noticed a species of flax in low grounds; the leaf, stem and pericarp resemble those of the common flax cultivated in the United States. The stem rises to a height of two and a half to three feet and spring to a number of eight or ten to the same root with a strong, thick bark apparently well calculated for use. The root seems to be perennial."

This perennial flax was so interesting that Lewis sent it back to Pursh with special comment, and Pursh, in acknowledgement, named it after the explorer. The plant furnished cords and a healing oil to the aborigines as well as to the explorers. The fibre, however, turned out to be less tough than that of the annual variety so Lewis' flax remains a wild flower.

LOCOWEED

Oxytropis

Before you have been long on the western prairies you will have become acquainted with the locoweed and the peculiar mental disorder it causes in cattle when they become 'loco' or crazy. The affection usually makes its appearance in spring and autumn when there is little nutritious grass for grazing. The disease is caused by feeding on one of three species of *Oxytropis* which are all found in our region. When the animal has acquired a taste for this plant it becomes an addict. No other food has any attraction. The disease is a nervous disorder finally resulting in mania, loss of sight and death from exhaustion — or starvation if the animal is removed from the supply of its beloved poison.

Oxytropis differs from the milk vetches (*astragalus*) in that the keel of the flower is tipped with a sharp-pointed appendage. The poisonous quality of the plant seems to vary with the locality. In some districts cases are quite common while in others the disorder is entirely absent. One writer suggests that the symptoms may result from barium poisoning from the soil rather than poisoning from the juice of the plant.

TOBACCO ROOT
Valeriana sitchensis

In moist meadows, clambering up the mossy banks of tumbling cascades or whitening the talus at the foot of a gaunt grey cliff, its sweet scented blossoms bowing to the ice-cooled winds, the valerian is one of the commonest flowers of the mountain regions. It is easily recognised by its strongly veined foliage and its clustered heads of

LOCOWEED

white or pinkish flowerets, looking soft and tousled because of the many long stamens. Another unmistakable characteristic is the thick rootstock with a strong disagreeable odour quite in contrast to the delicate odour of the flower.

One species has long fleshy taproots which were used as food by the western Indians either raw or dried, but their chief interest in the plant was for medicine. It was believed to be a cure for indigestion and

VALERIAN

disorders of the stomach, which must have been very prevalent amongst a people whose diet was so uncertain.

It has been found by modern scientists to contain a drug valuable in the treatment of nervous disorders.

Eastern nations use the root of a species of valerian for a costly perfume, which is not particularly agreeable to western tastes. It is believed that the precious ointment of spikenard mentioned in the Bible was made from this root.

ALUM ROOT

Heuchera ovalifolium

Because of its long spikes of closely set yellowish-white flowers which reach a height of twelve to twenty inches, the oval-leaved alum root is a conspicuous flower of the mountain slopes and the river valleys of the foothills. It is rather a handsome plant which is widely distributed throughout the west. In the mountains it makes itself a perfect rock garden plant, clinging to the sides of the canyons and precipices, outlining its white flowers against the dark purple rocks and thriving where moisture is scarce. It would be much more conspicuous and familiar to the average person were it not for the fact that it blooms at the season when the mountain slopes are as brilliantly coloured as a cloisonné enamel with flowers of every colour, shape and size, so that its many brilliant rivals quite over-shadow it.

The leaves are round with wavy margins and are clustered close to the ground leaving the flower stalks long and bare. In autumn they take on such a rich bronze-red colour that their fall garb attracts more attention than their springtime green and white.

The scaly root-stalks probably contain some of the same properties as alum salts. The Indians called it 'tastes dry' and used it for the treatment of haemorrhages as well as externally for sores and swellings. The true alum of familiar dry taste is used in medicine as an astringent and styptic.

Another Indian name for the plant is 'kalispell'.

BLUE FLAG

Blue flags, yellow flags, flags all freckled
Which will you take? Yellow, blue, speckled!
Take which you will, speckled, blue, yellow,
Each in its way has not a fellow.

Christina Rossetti

The flag or iris is a flower loved by the poets who have vied with each other through the centuries to invent beautiful words and to add to the symbolism clustered about its graceful personality. In poetry it has become the symbol of wisdom, truth and courage. Ruskin calls it the flower of chivalry, with a sword for its leaf and a lily for its heart.

Iris was a special winged attendant of Juno, usually represented seated behind her chariot robed in airy fabric of variegated hues. The rain-

BLUE FLAG

bow originally was regarded as the path over which she passed to earth and thus Iris became the personification of the rainbow. The flower acquired the name of iris because of its varied hues.

Centuries ago in France, it was adopted by Louis VII as the emblem of his house. The name 'Flower of Louis' became corrupted in the days of lax spelling to 'fleur-de-lis'.

It is found in low wet ground in the extreme southern part of Alberta, in Montana and across the prairie to Manitoba and North Dakota.

A big root-stalk insures food for the plant while it lies dormant under the winter ice and snow or when the moisture dries off at the end of the summer. This swollen root-stalk contains a powerful hepatic stimulant known as iridin.

A charming miniature sister of the blue flag, which is very common throughout the west, is the blue eyed grass.

VI. Dyes

"Of all God's gifts to the sight of man, colour is the holiest, the most divine, the most solemn."

John Ruskin

COLOUR IS all around us, in the skies, in the trees and in the flowers. But somehow, in the heart of man is a craving to have it even closer; to hold it in a vessel, to have power over it, to be able to change it at will; in other words, to create. And in order that his people might satisfy this craving, Old Man hid, in the oddest places about his garden, stores of all colours, from black to yellow and red.

The Indians first sought out these hidden dyes for use on their quills and feathers. Coal from the river banks, or chocolate-coloured stones, crushed and boiled with the bark of alder or hazel nut gave them their black. From the oregon grape and the dock they got their yellows. The fresh new leaves of the poplar, the mint and the glacier lily hid greens of varying shades. Their reds came from the roots of the bedstraw and gromwell and spruce, from cranberry, sorrel and cedar. Spruce bark and larkspur were sources of blues.

Most of these dyes were prepared in simple ways, generally by simmering the material with the dye-bearing plant. Modern dyers use alum to make materials receptive and acetic acid to bring out the colours; but the Indian women, having none of these at hand, found an efficient substitute in the acid juices of currents and gooseberries. The porcupine quills, when they were dyed, were rubbed with bear oil to give them that beautiful lustre which is one of their charms.

The enjoyment of vegetable dying today rests, not only in the pleasure of creating something from the ground up but also in the pleasant smells of the good earth and flowers that rise from the pot like incense.

A list of the sources of the various dyes reads like a description of a summer spent in the open:

Yellow
—the young leaves of the poplar, willow, alder, bracken, pine cones, yarrow, oregon grape, bog asphodel, ragwort, goldenrod

Red
—alder, bedstraw, gromwell, lamb's quarter, sorrel, cedar, cranberry, dogwood, hoary puccoon, St. John's-wort, spruce roots

Black
—alder boiled much longer than for red and yellow

Green
—bearberry, birch and equisetum

Purple
—blueberry, elder berry, or the roots of dandelion

Brown
—birch bark, juniper berry or hawthorn bark

Blue
—larkspur or spruce bark

Grey
—chokecherry

INDIAN PINK
Peritoma serrulatum

One of the commonest flowers of the prairie, found blooming in August along the roadsides and in waste places, is the Rocky Mountain bee plant, spider flower or Indian pink. It has a showy looking, bright pink, four-petalled flower, with long spidery stamens and lank pistil, carried in terminal racemes. As the flowers continue to open at the tips, the lower ones become long pendulous seed pods.

The whole plant, when boiled down, leaves a gummy brownish substance which the Indians of New Mexico allowed to dry into cakes of

INDIAN PINK

dye and stored. These cakes were soaked in water when needed and used for the brown decoration on their pottery.

On wool it makes a rather interesting greenish-grey.

Its one drawback is the vile smell of the boiling plant which is in such direct contrast to the delightful summer odours of goldenrod, birch leaves and other dye-producing plants.

NORTHERN BEDSTRAW

Galium

One of the most ancient dyes of our civilization is madder, obtained from the plant of the same name which is also known as *Rubia tinctorum* or 'dyer's root'. It was used for obtaining purples, browns and dull reds. In the seventeenth or eighteenth century an elaborate process was evolved which required three months or more of soaking the root in fat and mordanting in alum and lime water, whereby the now famous 'turkey red' was obtained from it. Madder is a native of the Mediterranean region, but it shows signs of becoming naturalized in some parts of Canada. Its flowers are small and bright yellow.

Native to the country, however, is a plant with a small white flower known as northern bedstraw, which possesses the same dye-producing root. It is a member of the madder family. There are some eighteen species of it, resembling each other so closely that they need not be dealt with separately. They grow throughout the continent from the Atlantic to the Pacific and north to the Arctic regions and are well enough known to have acquired almost seventy popular names. The commonest of these is cleavers, derived from the twin burrs of the seed with their numerous hooked bristles which attach themselves to passing objects.

Bedstraw is a smooth-stemmed perennial with many tiny four-parted white flowers and narrow leaves that grow in circles of three or four around the stem.

Sir John Franklin in *Polar Seas* describes how the Indians combined the roots of the northern bedstraw with the juice of strawberries and cranberries to obtain a beautiful scarlet. The plains Indians used it for colouring their porcupine quills.

NORTHERN BEDSTRAW

ALGAE

For certain greenish dyes, for decorations on buckskin and for paint-ing on their sacred tipis, the Indians used the scum from stagnant pools of the prairie. Since this scum on fresh-water pools is simply a mucila-ginous mass of tiny, rootless, leafless plants which belong to the very lowest strata of plant society, it is eligible for a place in this section on dye-producing plants.

In spite of their stemless, leafless condition these tiny plants are pos-sessors of the great gift of all plants, the ability to manufacture food from air, water and mineral salts, by the use of chlorophyll. They belong to the division known as algae, to which the sea-weeds also belong. Science traces the evolution of plant life from these tiny algae of fresh water ponds to spore-bearing mosses and ferns and from there to staminate and pistillate plants that reproduce by seed. The highest form of plant life yet evolved is believed to be the compositae group, in which many florets work together for the good of the community.

The colours of the hidden dyes have also evolved from the green of the algae to all the bright dyes of the flower world.

LICHENS

From the tiny algae of the ponds to the lichens of the mountain slopes is but a short step botanically. Some members of the algae group have agreed to a partnership with certain fungi, to form what the bota-nist knows as a lichen. To the algae, water is essential for life and repro-duction and fungi are great water gatherers, being able to absorb water from air so dry that nothing else could live in it. But the fungi are parasites, that is, they have been denied the chlorophyll-producing granules and so must obtain their food from other plants. So algae and fungi have gone into partnership, the algae providing the food and colour and the fungi providing the moisture. Thus the lichens can live on the bare trunks in dry forests or on barren sun-blistered rocks where no other life could exist.

This botanical partnership has furnished both the amateur and the commercial dyer with many of their most successful dyes. Harris, Shetland and Donegal tweeds are admired as much for their characteristic out-of-doors perfume, resulting from the lichen dyes used in their manufacture, as for the quality of their wools. Highland tartans have more charm than ever when we know that their crimsons and purples, their scarlets and yellows have come originally from lichens growing in woods and on rocky places; that their blacks are from alder, their magentas from the roots of the common dandelion and other shades of yellow from the roots of bracken.

The most famous of all the lichen dyes is one from which, by a process of fermentation, blue litmus solution is obtained, which may be turned red by adding an acid and blue again by adding an alkali.

The Indians did not miss this universal source of dye. In the dry pine forests of the mountain slopes, the lower branches of the trees are often covered with a bright yellow, branching lichen which may be gathered in generous quantities from the forest floor, where it has fallen after being loosened by the wind or birds from its slight hold on a rotting twig. This lichen, when boiled, produces a dye which the Indians used for porcupine quills and feathers and which is one of the simplest of colours for the amateur dyer to handle on wools. It produces a beautiful, clear yellow slightly tinged with green.

Lichens growing on stones may also be used and an even more brilliant colour is obtained from them than from those growing upon trees.

VII. Desert and Swamp

In the central part of the continent there is a region, desert or semi-desert in character, which can never be expected to become occupied by settlers. Although there are fertile spots throughout its extent it can never be of much advantage to us as a possession. Knowledge of the country as a whole would never lead me to advocate a line of communication.
Captain Palliser's Report, 1860

I fearlessly announced that the so-called arid country was one of unsurpassed fertility and that it was literally the 'Garden' of the whole country.
John Macoun, 1872

Arid Regions

ABOUT THE time when the first white men were making their perilous way across the dry plains of North America, a French scientist, Lamarck, as if to prepare the world for the study of the plants of this new country, advanced a theory that changed the whole trend of plant study. He suggested (a startlingly new idea for the times) that plants had learned, by a system of evolution, to adapt themselves to their environments.

In moist surroundings they have large leaves to help them get rid of excess moisture by transpiration. If, however, the moisture which the plant can absorb through its roots is less than the moisture which is given off by way of its leaves, the plant will wilt. Some plants attempt to prevent giving off too much by curling their leaves so that less of the surface is exposed to evaporation.

In dry sunny regions there is no such thing as excess moisture. The whole aim of the plants is to retain the moisture they have gathered, so they have small leaves, a soft coating of fine hairs, or a surface with a whitish bloom. The plants which grow on the prairie are those which have adapted themselves to prevent the loss of water by evaporation. Some of them are covered with minute scales that protect the sensitive breathing surface; others are grey and hairy; some have leaves that fold inward to hide the surface from the sun and others have decided to do without leaves altogether or to reduce them to the smallest dimensions possible. Most of them are perennials with deep tap roots which they send far into the depths of the soil, away from the sun and wind-dried surface. Some of these thirsty roots reach a depth of six or seven feet. This is no great accomplishment for a tree but is quite a feat for a small plant that does not stand more than a few inches in height.

PURPLE CACTUS

Neomammilaria vivipara

Of all the plants, the cactus has progressed farthest along the line of adaptation to drought conditions. To prevent loss of water by transpiration, it has reduced its leaves to scales or has dispensed with them altogether. It has built itself a system of reservoirs where it stores water for future use. These stores of water in a desert land made it attractive to animals, and so the plant was forced to increase its armaments. It surrounded itself with a whole forest of rapiers, which, be it said to its credit, are used strictly for self-defence and not as an excuse for carrying war into the territory of a weaker neighbour.

The purple cactus is one of those genera which occur only on the prairie. It is a very low growing plant, made up of clusters of stems that look like little round pin-cushions with all the pins arranged in painstaking designs, like the pins in the cushion in Grandmother's spare room. A reddish pin stands straight out from the centre of each tubercle, while white and red pins branch out from it to form a flat all-over pattern of radiating lines. The meticulous creator of this decorative pin-cushion, however, has placed all the pins with their points out, which makes the arrangement too painful to be practical except from the point of view of the plant, and has caused the plant to be called devil's pin-cushion. Its bloom is well worth waiting for even though it lasts so short a time. It would seem from the plants accredited to him in the west that the devil has a keen eye for beauty.

During the last hot days of the summer and throughout the long winter, the plant crouches low to the ground, looking grey and almost invisible against the brown grass, but with the coming of spring it puffs itself out, filling all its little tubercles with fresh green sap. In late June or early July, it is crowned with lovely bright glossy blooms having yellow centres and numerous rays of that singing magenta pink which nature uses so often for her early summer flowers. In the bright sun of noonday they open wide, measuring about one and a half or two inches across, but as soon as the sun grows cool, they close again to buds. Their blossoming turns the prairie pink for a day or two and then the colour is gone again for another year.

PURPLE CACTUS

A young plant consists of a single cushion or stem with two or three flowers. The older the plant grows, the more stems it develops and the more bloom it bears. One specimen produced nearly a hundred blossoms all open at once, on a clump that measured little more than a foot in diameter.

In the fall of the year, the plant produces a fleshy fruit which is as full of tiny seeds as a fig, and which has been used by enthusiastic home-makers for cactus jam.

PRICKLY PEAR
Opuntia polycantha

The yellow cactus or prickly pear, which turns the dry warm banks of so many prairie rivers into magnificent flower gardens for a few days in the early summer, belongs to a family celebrated for the food and drink they provided in the desert regions of the United States, as far south as Mexico where they are known as nopal and tuna. One of Luther Burbank's schemes was to develop a hybrid from this cactus that would be both spineless and edible.

In our territory, however, the plant is best known for the beauty of its yellow bloom and for its thorny disposition.

> "Our three persecutors, mosquitoes, gnats and prickly pear continue with us. The thorns are so strong that they pierce a double hide in parchment. Captain Clark's first employment, on lighting the fire, was to extract from his feet the briars, which he found seventeen in number."

The journals of all the prairie travellers are sprinkled with such complaints. Even the mild Captain Palliser, whose report is very dignified and official in its general tone, was moved to a sigh of remonstrance.

"Two other plants (besides sage) are in great abundance here, a small cactus and a stipa, both of which are sharp and poisonous, causing pain and irritation to the foot."

It was the custom of at least one tribe of Indians in the territory infested by the prickly pear, to remove their moccasins when smoking with a stranger, as an indication of the sincerity of their friendship.

The prickly pear plays a part in a well known Blackfoot legend. Once there were seven brothers who, with their little sister, were chased by a fearsome creature who possessed the magic power of becoming a woman or a bear at will. The eldest of the brothers had a magic feather. With it he could spread in this creature's pathway the three things that formed obstacles to travel in the Blackfoot country;

PRICKLY PEAR

first a mat of prickly pears, then a growth of thick underbrush, and finally a large sheet of water. But the bear-woman overcame all these obstacles and was about to capture them when they came to a tall tree which they climbed in haste. The four brothers who were lowest in the tree, unfortunately, fell off and in order to save them, the brother who possessed the powerful medicine shot an arrow into the skies, which carried them all out of reach of the bear-woman and pinned them against the sky forever. There you may see them tonight, the three boys and the little sister in the tree, and the other four boys lying as they fell from the tree. We call those seven stars the Big Dipper, but to the Blackfeet they are known as the Seven Brothers.

That civilized surroundings have not caused the cactus to reform its habits is amply demonstrated by the moans of amateur skiers on the steep banks of the prairie rivers, who have happened to sit down with sudden violence in a not too well planned location. The most effective remedy, so they say, is to spend the following week in the bath tub.

All this leads to the information collected by Walter McClintock, during his visits amongst the Indians, to the effect that the spines of the prickly pear were an effective cure for rheumatism. The spines were inserted into the flesh of the part affected and then were set afire, when they would burn to the very tip. No doubt the rheumatic pains would be immediately forgotten.

PRAIRIE MALLOW

Sphaeralcea coccinea

The prairie mallow is a low perennial, never growing much more than a foot high, usually less. Early in July, the grey-green mat of foliage along the roadsides of the prairie bursts into bloom, making a more brilliant display than any roadside plant except the sunflower. Its blooms measure about an inch across and grow in short racemes.

The petals are the colour of ripe tomatoes and tempted prairie children to call it tomato flower.

It belongs to dry plains and sandy valleys but loves the freshly dug earth of the roadside, clinging to the straight cut-banks and making a green hedge along many of the graded roads. In the days when Bourgeau was making his enthusiastic collection of prairie flowers, this beautiful red mallow won his admiration. It chose the same sort of location, along the steep earthy banks of the roads that criss-crossed the prairie. That these banks were cut by the sharp hooves of the buffalo in their daily wanderings seemed to matter little to the plant.

This bright blossom makes a very satisfactory garden plant for a sunny situation. It is not such an enthusiastic grower that it will become a nuisance, but is very showy during its blooming season of two or three weeks and the grey clump of foliage is decorative when the bloom is gone.

PRAIRIE MALLOW

PRAIRIE CLOVER

Petalostemon

In early summer, flowers of every colour form a variegated carpet over hundreds of miles of plain country. Of these none are more showy in mass or more beautiful individually than the prairie clovers.

The purple prairie clover is an upright plant from one to three feet high. It is one of those dry region plants which has almost dispensed with leaves. They are short and very narrow, with the edges rolled inward to protect the delicate breathing surface. The flowers are carried in a short dense spike which is first a cone of grey silky buds arranged spirally. The lower buds open first, the circle of flowers moving gradually upward towards the tip. So closely packed are these little flowers that they form a compact feathery cluster of magenta-pink petals with numerous long, conspicuous orange stamens. The stems, like those of most drought-loving plants, are heavy and woody, covered with grey down and sometimes stained with red as if the colouring matter of the petals had overflowed along them.

The heads of these plants retain their colour and form when dried. With everlastings, they make an interesting winter bouquet.

Prairie clover is one of the fifteen genera which are confined to the prairie regions of this continent. It is a bit difficult to reconcile its name with its appearance since it is very different from the popular conception of a clover. The botanist, however, bases his classification on the arrangement of the vital organs rather than the outward appearance of the plant and so this unusual looking flower has qualified for membership in the pea family.

There are four varieties found in our territory, of which the purple is the most common. There is also a very common white variety which is found in dense mats along the sandy banks of the rivers.

PRAIRIE CLOVER

SKELETON WEED

Lygodesmia juncea

Between the hairy, grey-leaved plants of the dry regions and the leaf-less, bulbous-stemmed cacti, is the queerest plant of the arid regions. It

is known as the skeleton weed or prairie pink. The stems are fat and very grey; the leaves are reduced to a minimum and are formed like tiny bracts; the florets, though numerous in other plants of the same family, are limited to five. The pale pink, rather attractive flowers, which open in the hottest sunshine, last but a short time.

This flower, more than any other, should have warned men against ploughing up the prairie of the dust bowl region and planting the shallow rooted crops which were easily destroyed by winds and shifting earth. With deep thick roots, scanty foliage and even a minimum of petals, it has adapted itself to the hard life which was too much for the softer grains.

SKELETON WEED

SAGE

Artemisia

Day after day the pioneers looked out over flat prairie covered with endless miles of dull grey sage. The sun rose over grey sage in the morning and set over grey sage at night. The moon shone down on the grey sage plain. The sound of the sage was in the wind and the smell of sage hung heavy during the infrequent rains. And the pioneers hated it or wrote songs about it according to their dispositions.

In an English garden a clump of sage is grown for its dainty, feathery foliage and its rich odour in wet weather. Visitors exclaim over its beauty. The gardener loves it because it whispers to him stories of great dry plains and buffalo herds, of trains of oxen and covered wagons, gold rushes and new railroads, Indian battles and lonely pioneers. To him it is a 'magic feather' that waves the way to adventure.

The Indians who lived amongst it as steadily as the pioneer named it 'magic feather' and were not blind to its beauty and character. The Blackfeet considered it one of their most sacred plants and used it in many of their ceremonies. They also tied it to articles which were sacrificed to the sun—a very beautiful and appropriate bit of symbolism, for what plant belongs more completely to the sun than the prairie sage?

Amongst some prairie tribes it played an important part in the Sun Dance ceremony. The young men who were about to take part in the dance were laid upon a bed of sage while the thongs were fastened under the muscles of their breasts.

However much the sage brush seems to belong to the west, it was well known to botanists long before America was drawn upon a map. The scientific name of sage is *artemisia*. It was so named in honour of the beautiful wife of King Mausolus, who has added the word 'mausoleum' to our language, because of the magnificent tomb she built in memory of her husband.

A plant with such a healing, stimulating smell must obviously find its way into many medicine kits. Pliny mentions it in his *Natural History* as a restorer of youth, if placed under the pillow at night. It was grown in English gardens under the name of 'old man', but as it was often used for a vermifuge it was also called 'wormwood'. A bitter aromatic liquor, *crème d'absinthe,* was made from its leaves. In the list of simples known to mountain climbers, sage tea is recommended as a stimulant to the action of the heart and as a restorer of energy. The Indians used it as a cure for mountain fever.

SCARLET GAURA

Its aromatic tang, which makes it so unpopular with bees has suggested its use as a substitute for moth balls.

There are some two hundred species of *artemisia* listed in world botanies. In his *Flora of the Prairies and Plains,* P. A. Rydberg has described over thirty.

SCARLET GAURA

Gaura coccinea

The scarlet gaura or butterfly weed is a species confined to the prairie region. As is often the case with prairie species, the leaves are grey and numerous but small. The stems are much branched and reclining, growing to a height of from six inches to a foot or more.

It shares with its tall brilliant relatives of the tropics the strange habit of opening four pure white petals and dying them first pink and then scarlet, as the sun warms them, so that on a single flower stalk one may find blossoms ranging from pure white to vivid scarlet.

The four petals are set on a much prolonged, brightly coloured calyx tube. Adding to the beauty of the flower itself are the eight long, showy, red-tipped stamens.

The Swamp

The sun, though it shines with all the intensity in its power, is never taken to the heart of the swamp as it is to the heart of the desert. Underneath the sun-warmed surface is always the cold, black opaqueness of the slime—part water, part loam, part decaying vegetable matter—always waiting to seize the unwary traveller, to swallow him, to hide him forever from the world.

The Indians were afraid of these places. With all the wealth of the prairies at hand, they had no need of a swamp, and it is no wonder that they peopled it with awesome creatures, man-eaters and ghosts, who swallowed people who were foolhardy enough to venture into its depths. Even the vapour which is so often seen to hover over moist or swampy places they believed to be the spirit of some person lately dead.

In these awesome surroundings live all the left-overs from an ancient time, all the strange freaks of plant society that have, somehow, managed to escape the oblivion that was the fate of the dinosaurs, ammonites and other creatures of their forgotten world.

Here, about the borders of the swamp, even along most ponds and ditches for that matter, can be found remnants from all the long aeons of plant history. Here is the scum upon the water, the lowest form of plant life which, scientists believe, belonged to the first stratum of the earth's crust, although here geologists have found no clue to existing life. Even in the second period, life is known to have existed only because in that stratum are found carboniferous shales and limestone deposits.

From the earliest forms of plant life, which reproduced by a breaking up of cells, plant society advanced to reproduction by spores, or by very small grains upon the leaves or in specially arranged cups. By the middle of the third period of earth history geologists first find traces of ferns and club mosses and other spore-bearing plants, which, by the end of the era had covered the land with forests as high as trees.

After the era of the spore bearers, came conifers and cycads or palm-like plants which bear naked seeds or cones.

Aeons later came one of the most striking developments in the evolution of plants. In the Cretaceous period, the latter part of which was the coal period of western North America, the sea spread across the continent, almost on a level with the swampy land and narrow inlets. On ridges of sand, between great marshes, grew red-woods, maples, poplars, sequoias, figs and other trees. Great marshy plains were covered with giant reeds and grasses, through which wandered horned, plated and carnivorous dinosaurs. But most important of all, from the point of view of plants, was the appearance on earth for the first time of flowering plants—plants which bear flowers and reproduce by seed. Grasses also had their origin in this period and all plants that support animal life flourished.

These flowers and grasses, with figs and palm leaves, dropped in the soft sand, mingling with the teeth and bones of strange reptiles and fishes as well as rushes and other aquatic plants. They were covered again by the sea, and then, for aeons, by the great fields of ice of the Glacial period, which gouged and changed and modelled the land again, covering the ancient swamps with a layer of yellow silt—the silt which, today, lies many hundreds of feet thick, over most of the western world. It is only where modern rivers have cut deep into this glacial deposit that figs are found and stumps of trees, the bones of dinosaurs and giant tracks moulded into the rocks. Here also the very first forms of flowering plants are found, fossilized, beside the blooming compositae of the Age of Man. To the stratum above the silt of the Glacial Period belongs the Age of Man—so recent is his history beside the history of the flowers.

ERA	PERIOD	
ANTHROPOZOIC	Recent and Prehistoric	Bright petalled flowers and compositae groups
	Pleistocene	
KAINOZOIC	Glacial	Ice Age — the most recent period before the Age of Man
	Pliocene	
	Miocene	
	Oligocene	
	Eocene	
MESOZOIC	Upper Cretaceous	Plant life began to assume a modern aspect — appearance of birch, beech, oak, walnut, maple, palms; also grasses
	Lower Cretaceous	Flowers — appearance and development of angiosperms
	Jurassic	Slow progress towards types which exist today — cycads and conifers
	Triassic	Dynosaurs
PALAEOZOIC	Permian	New types of the group which include the giant sequoia
	Upper Carboniferous	Gymnosperms in abundance. Forests of horse-tails and ferns
	Lower Carboniferous	Earliest wood growing in rings
	Devonian	Origin of ferns, gigantic horse-tail rushes and club mosses
	Silurian	
	Ordovician	Meagre record of plants
	Cambrian	Sponges and corals
PRETEROZOIC		First sign of life
ARCHAEOZOIC	Pre-Cambrian	No clue to life

MOSSES AND LICHENS

The first plants to appear on bleak unfriendly rocks, where no other plant can find a foothold, are the mosses and lichens. "The orange stain which is Time's finger mark on the grey wall", seems to appear as if by magic.

"Spontaneously, inorganic stone became living plant", the philosophers of a century ago were wont to explain. But all that carefully evolved theory was ruined by Pasteur, Lister and their fellow scientists. However, the newer theory that mosses and lichens were the first plants to cover the earth's surface and that they and the grey rocks had the earth to themselves for an aeon or two seems less vulnerable.

Mosses and lichens are both soil makers, breaking the surface of stones into minute particles in their search for mineral salts, or reclaiming the waters of a lake, spreading their carpets of moss across it, filling it with earth mould and giving foothold to larger plants who help them with their work.

This they did for the rocks and waters of the archaic world, taking thousands of years to prepare the soil for the conifers and flowers.

They repeated their efforts after the Ice Age in North America. As the great ice sheets melted, they left in their wake many lakes and ponds, the smaller of which the peat moss claimed as its own. Any sheets of water not over a mile in extent, on which the waves could not become too boisterous, were favourable quarters for their work. And so they laid a second carpet as a pathway for the trees and flowers.

Now the same cycle occurs again on the mountain tops. A lake is seized by sphagnum moss, converted into a bog, and then into a forest floor. Or a lichen, blown to a rocky slope, ekes out a living on the barren rock, making a bed for the spores of mosses. The moss grows and spreads and greedy seeds of angiosperms seize the bit of foothold, and revel in the water the moss has stored. So the shale slopes, at an altitude of nine thousand feet, are patched with little discs of green, some not a

foot across, but already blossoming with as many as ten varieties
of flowers.

One has to live with the mosses and lichens to become acquainted
with them. They are elusive little things, changing form and colour
with every change of atmosphere. A sudden rain may change a dry
brown bank to a soft green cushion, or a dead grey disc to shining
green. Mosses have learned to fold their leaves for the retaining of moisture. Clumps of sphagnum moss and reindeer lichen which appear to
be completely dry on top, often have, concealed underneath, enough
moisture for a man to drink.

MANNA IN THE WILDERNESS

The story of the manna which fell from the skies to feed the Israel-
ites is one of those miracles which has been explained by science and
yet remains as much of a miracle as ever. In Algeria and Tartary, as
well as in other mountainous countries, there is a lichen whose oval,
warted crust is edible. It is known to the Tartars as earth bread. Having
but a loose foothold on the mountain slopes, it is easily torn off and
carried to the plain below by the winds which sweep through the valleys. At times, we are told, this strange rain accumulates to the depth of
several inches and is used in parts of the southwest of Asia as a substitute for corn.

Through most temperate regions these small weird plants are curiosi-
ties or are used for the luxuries of dyes or medicines, but in Arctic regions they again assume a dominant position in the economy of the human race. Travellers in these zero regions, where fire is a necessity and
trees are non-existent, find fuel growing on the stony hilltops. Reindeer moss, which is almost white, and another moss which is black,
furnish when dry the only fuel of the country. These mosses, together
with rock tripe, a species of edible lichen, are credited with once having saved the life of Sir John Franklin when he was reduced to starvation in the Arctic regions.

Captain Palliser found the Wood Crees using as their principal foods small fruits such as cherries and saskatoons, and a lichen from a species of pine tree.

Daniel Harmon, a partner of the North West Company at the beginning of the nineteenth century, records that the natives in many parts of the west were frequently obliged to subsist on a kind of 'moss' which they found adhering to the rocks, and which they called As-se-ne Wa-quon-uck, that is, eggs-of-the-rock. On the Columbia River, where he was in charge of a trading post for several years, near the headwaters of the Saskatchewan, he found the natives subsisting during the greater part of the summer upon roots and a kind of dry bread made of

> "the mossy stuff which grows on the spruce-fir tree and which resembles cobwebs, spun by spiders. This substance contains a little nourishment. They gather it from the trees and lay it in a heap, on which they sprinkle a little water and leave it to ferment. After that they roll it up into balls as large as a man's head, and bake them in the oven, well heated, which is constructed in the earth, where it is baked one hour."

By this 'moss which resembles cobwebs', he probably means the lichen of the genus *Unsea* which is popularly known as old man's beard and is common on pine trees, both living and dead, throughout the region.

HORSE-TAILS

Equisetum

With the fossilized forms of dinosaurs and other prehistoric animals are found perfectly preserved specimens of giant horse-tails. They grew in dense forests, attaining a girth of three feet and a height of from sixty to ninety feet.

There are ten or more species of descendants of these antediluvian giants growing in our territory today, none of them more than two or three feet in height. The plant is flowerless and is allied to the ferns and club mosses. In some species the stem is straight and unbranched, while in others it carries slender branches in whorls, which give the plant the appearance of a miniature evergreen. The stems are rough, round and ridged. The leaves are merely scales borne in rings around the green stems. The fertile stems, which appear in the early spring, are light brown and bear the spores in cones at the top. The fertile cone is covered with small circular spore-bearing scales. The spore itself has four small threads or 'elators' coiled about it like a spring, which, expanding suddenly, throw the spore from its resting place on the cone.

Joint grass is another name for the plant, given because the stems are divided into sections by large and easily separated joints. In Europe it is used by the peasants for scrubbing floors and has there been given the name of scouring rush.

The Indians found very different uses for it, boiling it in water for a drink and using it for horse medicine. Apparently its taste appeals to animals, for if you should see a moose standing knee-deep in a swampy lake, his mouth full of dripping greens, the chances are that he is intent on a meal of *equisetum*.

The Palliser party found that their horses fattened on the *equisetum* found along the swampy borders of the foothill ponds. More than once, as Sir James

HORSE-TAILS

Hector made his perilous way through the forests of the Kicking Horse Pass, the only food the horses had was a few blades of this same plant.

CLUB MOSS
Lycopodium

Sharing the luxuriance of the Carboniferous period with the giant ferns and horse-tails, were giant club mosses. Their descendants are found today in the woods of the mountains, as much reduced from the size of their forbears as the present day horse-tails.

They are called mosses but are really a step above the mosses in evolution, as they possess tubular cells for the carrying of liquid from one part of the plant to another and have also roots or underground organs with carrying cells. A special family has been created for them known as *Lycopodium* or club moss.

The club mosses are low growing moss-like plants, only a few inches high, with numerous tiny leaves resembling those of cedars and firs. The spores (for they belong to an era long before seed-bearing plants appeared) are borne, either in the axils of the leaves, or in cup-shaped fruit spikes, formed of leaves which are very different from those of the sterile branches. Their resemblance to cedars and firs has given them such common names as ground cedar and running pine. They are not to be confused with the creeping cedar or juniper which has a cone-like berry of pale blue, and belongs to the order of trees rather than mosses.

Some of these club mosses hold, on their Christmas tree foliage, erect little cylindrical spikes like Christmas candles. Perhaps this accounts for their other popular name of Christmas greens.

SUNDEW

One of the strangest of the small carnivora of the swamp and indeed of the whole plant world is the sundew, about which enough has been written to fill a library. Darwin, who considered it the most wonderful plant in the world, devoted half a book to telling about his experiments with it.

The plant first tempts an insect with a sweet, sticky juice that holds its feet and makes escape difficult. The moment the insect begins to struggle the stiff hairs of the leaf spring like a trap to seize it and the leaf bends around it. So closely does the leaf enfold the struggling insect that its form may be seen through the leaf. With a strong juice the plant digests the part it needs, then opens again to wait for another victim. If the insect is too small or does not contain the substance necessary to its diet, however, the leaf opens again immediately allowing the alien matter to drop away.

Should you feel a lack of friendship, it might be worth a trip to the swamp to gather a leaf of the sundew. Mediaeval writers gravely assure their readers that a leaf carried in the pocket will protect the bearer from witchcraft and ensure friendship.

BUTTERWORT
Pinguicula vulgaris

Along the borders of the swamp, or clinging to sheer rocks that are continually moistened by spray from a dashing stream, grows a miniature ogre of the plant world. Often called moss violet, it is in reality not even connected with the violet family, although no one could be blamed for mistaking it for one. The flower of the butterwort, for such is its name, is very like a large rich purple violet. At the base of the stems, however, in the place of the usual violet leaves, there is a rosette of greasy, succulent, yellow-green leaves, covered with glandular hairs on which is secreted a colourless fluid.

When a small insect alights on the leaf, it is held by the sticky surface. The edge of the leaf rolls up to prevent its escape. The irritation causes the glands to become more active and the fluid becomes more generous and more acid. The acid digests the animal matter, the plant absorbs the resultant fluid and the leaves unroll themselves in readiness for the next victim. In this way the plant gets its supply of nitrogen which is usually lacking in the wet places that it inhabits.

Peasants in Ireland used the acid leaves in cheese making.

BUTTERWORT

BLADDERWORT

Utricularia

Such a strange little monster as the bladderwort seems to belong to the mouldering surface of a hidden forest bog, rather than to the honest sunlight of a prairie pool, but it is at home, from one coast to the other, wherever there is a still pool or slow running ditch.

A bright yellow, attractive little flower, somewhat like a snapdragon, with a puffed up throat and a small spur, looks up at you from the surface of the pond. You stoop to pick it and find in your hand a whole dripping network of greenish slimy threads, two feet or more in length. These threads are the leaves, which are fine to reduce their resistance to the water. They branch from three long stems that spread out in the water to support the plant.

The strangest part of the entire plant is the collection of translucent bladders ranged along the stem at the joints of the leaves. The plant gets its scientific name from *utriculus,* the Latin for 'little bag.' These little bags are provided with trap doors that open in but not out.

If a specimen is lifted from the water and is placed in a pan, frantic activity will be noticed among the leaves. The water will be found to be full of little animals, fresh water shrimps for the most part, with silvery translucent bodies which turn shrimp pink in death. These are the fortunate crustaceans which have been spared the death that threatened them in the bladderwort's little bags. For the plant feeds on the minutest crustaceans, gnat larvae and so on, that inhabit the pond. They are drawn through the trap door into the pods, where they die a slow death in their little prison, and are converted into soup for the consumption of the plant, the juice alone being used.

In the autumn, the buds at the ends of the floating stems fall off and sink into

BLADDERWORT

the mud below, and when spring comes they sprout and branch. The bladders are filled with water until the plant is ready to bloom. Then they fill with air, like miniature balloons, and carry the plant to the surface. These bladders have still another use; when the pond dries up they retain water enough to keep the plant living for some time.

CANCER ROOT and
INDIAN PIPE

INDIAN PIPE AND CANCER ROOT

While on the subject of miscreants and oddities let us also mention ghouls. The Indian Pipe, one of the oddest plants, has an individuality all its own. It is leafless and has no green colour, though at times it is bluish or pinkish and it turns black when dying. A parasite, it feeds on roots of other plants or on decaying matter of the forest floor. Cold and clammy, it is the ghost that walks the forest aisles. The straight stem and nodding bell-shaped flower imitates the shape of a pipe.

We usually connect such parasites with shadowy places but there is one at least that carries on its thieving in the open sunlight of the prairie or mountain slopes. It lives on the roots of the eriogonum, phacelia, sage and other members of the compositae family.

When the seed sprouts it produces a tiny root, which grows and branches underground, until it touches a suitable root or 'host'. Then it sends out a sucker, which attaches itself to the root. The plant grows and develops underground until it is ready to bloom. It then sends up a stem, from one to four inches high, on which are purplish or yellowish flowers. The leaves, lacking chlorophyll, are unable to fulfill their duty as food producers, and so have been reduced to mere brownish scales. The seeds are small and numerous. The plant, above ground, is a pink or grey-red unhealthy looking, fleshy affair, that suits well the names of cancer root and ghost pipes.

In spite of the rather unwholesome appearance of the plant, the Indians used it as an application for the healing of wounds.

GRASS OF PARNASSUS

Parnassia

Grass of Parnassus is a beautiful, ethereal creature, whose open-faced innocence masks a coldly calculating nature. She has an easily appeased conscience that does not hesitate over false advertising and deception. And there is no fatherly government or tradesmen's code to protect the victims from her deceit.

The flower is made up of five snowy petals delicately veined with green. Near the base of each is a fan-shaped arrangement of filaments, each of which is neatly tipped with a transparent yellow bead that looks like pure nectar.

"Aha", says the bee on seeing it, "Here is a feast fit for a god, laid out where it can be reached without all this digging and delving into the depths of a flower." He immediately attempts to regale himself with the tempting globules only to find that they are false, like the cardboard cakes in the confectioner's window. Each shining drop is made of wood.

But alighting for this feast, the insect fertilizes the cone-shaped ovary which is topped with four stigmas, and brushes the stamens which are placed alternately with the petals, so carrying the pollen to the next flower.

There seems to be no satisfactory explanation of either part of the common name.

There are several varieties of grass of Parnassus, all with the same clustered basal leaves and solitary flowers. A fringed variety is quite

GRASS OF PARNASSUS

common, and in the mountains grows a dwarf species, only a few inches high, which is found as far north as the Barren Lands and is also a denizen of high mountain peaks where similar conditions prevail.

YELLOW POND LILY

Nymphaea polysepala

On the brown surfaces of still ponds across the country float the yellow bowls of the pond lily. A distinctly western species is Nymphaea polysepala or many sepalled water-nymph. Two other types are found in our region but all are so similar that the differences matter only to the scientist. The scientific name Nymphaea came to us from the

Greeks who appropriately dedicated the plant to the nymphs of fountain and lake.

The showiest part of the flower is the calyx which consists of numerous rounded, concave sepals, coloured yellow, usually tinged with red. The petals are small and inconspicuous, resembling stamens. The handsome foliage, light and full of air, floats on the surface of the water on long stalks which rise from the muddy bottom. The fruit contains a great number of small shiny seeds which grow heavy as they ripen and drop to the bottom of the pond.

These seeds are highly nutritious and were gathered by the Indians of the northwest. Roasted on top of the fire like popcorn or ground into flour much like the corn flour of the south, they formed a staple food which the Klamath Indians called 'wokas'.

YELLOW POND LILY

SWAMP PERSICARIA
Persicaria muhlenbergii

Swamp persicaria is also commonly known as rosy polygonum (*Polygonum muhlenbergii*). It is closely related to the bistorts but it sets its roots in the mud at the bottom of swamps or shallow pools, rather than growing on their banks.

Its beautiful rose-coloured spikes light up the margins of a dark forest pool or the surface of a wayside pond. 'Lake margin's pride' Emerson called it with reason. It is one of the prettiest aquatic plants of the plain and lower mountains.

The flowers are small, in a terminal raceme, the calyx providing the colour. The stems are channelled and enlarged at the points from which grow the leaves, which gives rise to the common name of knotweed which has been applied to many members of the family. *Polygonum,* in fact, in Greek means 'many-kneed' and refers to the large joints. The leaves are oblong, pointed at the apex, and rounded at the base. At times they float on the surface, at others they are immersed beneath the water.

VIII. Incense

I know
That if odour were visible as colour is, I'd see
The summer garden aureoled in rainbow clouds.
Robert Bridges

SWEET GRASS

LET us stop for a while in a green prairie meadow. Let us sink down into the tall grass and listen to its whisperings. Perhaps if we shut our eyes and are very quiet we may see, down vistas of time, a younger prairie, clean and vital, when men, animals and flowers lived together as friends; when midnight stars looked down on whispering groups outside the tipis, on brown figures crouched to gleaming fires; when Sun blazed down on a worshipping people and strode, the magnificent god of the prairie, across his great blue lodge.

In yonder tipi see a reverent and silent group. A tall figure, rising, approaches the little fire burning in the centre. With red-painted willow tongs he lifts a gleaming coal, placing it with reverence upon an altar. From a pouch he takes a finger full of grass and lays it on the coal. A wisp of sweetly scented smoke floats upward and hovers under the roof. The crouching figures rise and bathe their hands in the smoke. A sacred song is sung. Then the chief with solemn dignity unrolls the sacred bundle. Each soft tanned wrapping is, in turn, held over the sweet grass incense until, from within the folds, is drawn the sacred pipe—a long slender tube hung with eagle plume, ermine and beautiful bright feathers. It in turn is held in the sacred incense and the ceremony of the medicine pipe continues with singing and dancing. Then as solemnly the pipe is placed again in its wrappings, with bundles of sweet grass and sacred tobacco, against the next using.

See also, a medicine woman in a lodge where a man lies sick. With willow tongs she lifts a coal to the altar, places on it a wisp of grass, and in the incense bathes her hands, praying that they may be given power to find the cause of the illness.

There is a camp sweet with saskatoon blossoms. It is the time of the ceremony of the planting of the sacred tobacco. Each man who takes part is purified in sweet grass incense—each one chews a piece and lays it on his head and body.

SWEET GRASS

Out there by the edge of the mountains is a solitary camp where a man is bathing in the smoke of the sweet grass. Seizing the smoke in both his hands he rubs it over his body. Before dawn he will go to his eagle pit and he must give off no man scent or the wily birds will not approach near enough for him to catch them. Far away, another lonely man is burning sweet incense to draw his dream helper to him before he goes to sleep, for sweet grass has many magic powers.

Sweet grass once lived in the sky. It came to earth through a hole in the blue lining of the Sun Chief's lodge —a hole that we call the North Star— through which shines the light of the fire in the Sun Chief's lodge. The hole was made when an Indian maiden (could she have known Eve?) pulled up the sacred turnip which Sun had forbidden her to touch.

Morning Star had seen this maiden first in the Blackfoot camp on the prairie and had loved her so that he took her to the sky to live with him. She was very happy there until she was tempted (by a serpent in the form of a pelican) to pull the forbidden plant. Through the hole she saw her home again far down against the prairie. Sun, at the same time angry and pitying, sent her back to her people and with her she brought to earth the sacred turnip, the sweet grass and a root digger painted red. When the grass had grown and the prairie was well covered with it, Sun sent another messenger to the people telling them many things. He sent them the songs and ceremonies of the Sun Dance. He told them how to purify themselves outwardly by the use of the sweet grass incense and inwardly by nibbling the sacred turnip.

Because of its strong sweet odour, the sweet grass was worn by the Indians in long, heavy braids around their necks. At one time it was very popular for small baskets and household articles in the homes of the early west, but now our baskets come from elsewhere and this use for the sweet grass seems almost forgotten.

Let us leave the sweet grass now in its sunny meadow and retreat hastily lest its fine spirit receive a crushing blow; for its portrait, life-size, is in a book here by my side, entitled *Noxious Weeds of Alberta*.

TOBACCO
Nicotiana quadrivalvis

The smoking of the calumet or pipe of peace by the natives of the new world was the first ceremonial to interest the earliest visitors to eastern shores and the ceremony was equally as significant on the western prairies. The bowls of these pipes were usually made of red stone which was found in quarries in certain parts of the country. Amongst the tribes of long ago, these quarries were sanctuaries where the most bitter enemies might meet in safety and peace.

The pipe stems were made of hard wood, often of elder. The stems of the ceremonial pipes were as much as four or five feet long and elaborately decorated with porcupine quills, strips of ermine and feathers.

At the beginning of every ceremony, however simple, the pipe was filled with sacred tobacco and a whiff of smoke was sent first upward to Sun and downward to the Earth Person; then a puff was blown in all four directions, east, south, west and north.

It was no ordinary tobacco that was used in these pipes but a hallowed plant whose seeds had been presented to the remote ancestors of each tribe in various miraculous ways. Most of the tribes of the plains connected the origin of the seeds, the sacred pipe and the ceremonial bundle invariably accompanying it with the Beaver, a much revered animal in many Indian doctrines. The story is briefly outlined in some of its variations.

The Legend of the Beaver

The younger brother of a chief was dipping water on the shores of Waterton Lake (or St. Mary's Lake or the Saskatchewan River) when a beaver appeared and invited him to come to the beavers' lodge. The young man did as he was invited and soon found himself in the beavers' underwater lodge. The old beaver, usually white, then showed him a sacred pipe and a skin of every animal on earth and taught him songs and dances to accompany each skin as it was unrolled from the bundle. Finally, from the very heart of the bundle, he gave the young man the seeds of the tobacco plant, describing to him all the ceremonies which must accompany the planting of them. The young brave returned to his people with the bundle, and after purifying himself in the incense from some sweet scented plant, he taught his people all that he had learned.

Each spring this bundle was opened and the seeds planted with elaborate and symbolic ceremony. All summer as the tribes roamed the prairie in search of winter supplies, prayers were offered for the safe keeping of this important crop and in the fall the leaves were cut and seeds restored to the bundle for use the following spring. This tobacco is listed in the botanies as a wild flower of our territories, though it has never become very common. Farther south, however, where the summers are longer and the winters not quite so cold, it flourished, and as the tribes gradually became careless of their rituals, it was acquired from the neighbouring tribes by trading.

According to J. W. Schultz, the Blackfeet clung until quite recent years to their seeds and ceremonies, hiding their tobacco plantations amongst the clumps of willows on their reserve at Gleichen. The description of this beautiful and symbolic ceremony is well worth reading. It may be found in *Sun God's Children,* by J. W. Schultz and J. L. Donaldson.

DOG-FENNEL

Chamomilla suaveolens

"Do you like pineapple? Then smell these."

This was the greeting given to each new visitor to our pineapple patch out behind the garage where no one ever troubled to weed. And

DOG-FENNEL

sure enough, the little insignificant weed that we picked smelled just like pineapple freshly cut.

This graceful odour is all the plant has to recommend it. Its flower clusters are little rayless cones looking like small yellow-green gum drops on a green stem surrounded with feathery, fern-like foliage.

Lewis and Clark exclaimed about the beauty of the great showy flowers in their path, but they did not miss the humblest weed. They gathered this small sweet-scented flower in Idaho and Pursh gave it a name based on its distinguishing feature—*Chamomilla suaveolens*. In other works it is probably better known as *Matricaria matricarioides*.

It is closely related to the chamomile of Grandmother's medicine chest and was often used by pioneers to replace it. But the Blackfeet had a much better idea—from the point of view of the patient at least. They dried the blossoms and placed them in their buckskin bags for perfume.

IX. Moon-of-the-Flowers

I envy not the rich their fields
Nor councillors their power,
While all the world my palace is
And every weed a flower.

Roundelay

In China, we are told a flower presides over each month of the year, but because there are many flowers and only a very few months, one day of the year is set aside as the birthday of all the flowers. On this day, gifts of seeds and slips are carried to one's friends and parties given in honour of the flowers. Wealthy families often give magnificent flower shows. The gown worn to such a party must be delicate in colour, and fashioned on simple lines. It is to celebrate the flowers that the people are gathered, and to wear a gown that distracts attention from the flowers is considered bad taste.

In the west, during the Moon-of-the-flowers, this custom is reversed. It is the flowers who are the hosts. They spread the hills and plains with a magnificent display, and every one who owns a car, a carriage or even two good feet, goes out at some time to dine with them. By the roadside, amongst the trees, everywhere, are little piles of blackened rocks where kettles have been boiled. One suspects, however, that these guests do not always show the exquisite courtesy shown in China or it would not be necessary for governments to carry on such extensive campaigns for the preservation of the wild flowers.

RED LILY

Lilium montanum

I took a day to search for God
And found him not.
But where the scarlet lily flamed
I saw his footprint in the sod.

Bliss Carman

When the red lily blooms, spring is over and summer in all its glory has arrived. Thoreau associates it with the spirit of summer and places it as the central figure in his landscape of that season.

> "The red lily with its torrid colour and sun freckled spots, dispensing too with the outer garment of a calyx, its petals so open and wide apart that you can see through it in every direction, tells of hot weather. It belongs not to the spring."

Not a famous writer like Thoreau, the botanist John Macoun has nevertheless drawn as fine a picture of the summer as he saw it when crossing the plains west of Qu'Appelle in 1879.

> "Sometimes lilies are so abundant that they cover an acre of ground bright red. At others they are mixed with other lilaceous plants such as *Zygadenus glaucus,* and form a ring around the thickets which we passed. Another time we came upon a pool of fine, pure water and in it grew *Carex aristata,* which the horses love so well. Outside of these a ring of white anemones and, as the ground becomes still drier, *Pentstemon confertus* would appear and lastly lilies would surround the whole."

The red lily has been chosen the provincial floral emblem for Saskatchewan.

The Indians of the upper Fraser River used the root of this lily, a bulb composed of narrow, jointed, fleshy scales, as an article of food.

Carefully steamed, it was considered by the early travellers as an excellent substitute for the potato. The flavour was reported by some to be like roasted chestnut with a slight but agreeable bitterness. But there was, as usual, another point of view. Dr. Cheadle's companion, Lord Milton, bought some of the bulbs from the Indians near the present site of Kamloops and Dr. Cheadle mentions them in his diary:

> "Being very bitter it quite spoiled our rubaboo (a stew made by boiling a piece of pemmican in a large quantity of water thickened with flour). Milton, of course, swore it was delicious."

In my search for legends of the wild flowers, tales of this most universally known and admired flower have eluded me. A Manitoban was

RED LILY

so anxious to have a story about her favourite flower included that she decided to remedy the oversight by writing one herself. She says:

> Once a little dappled fawn
> Stood beside a pool at dawn.

He was wishing the glorious orange-red of the sunrise might be spread throughout the day. His wish was granted when the beautiful red lilies appeared in the grass.

> Colours of the fawn they hold
> And of the sunrise, red and gold.

Perhaps there are many stories which have not yet come my way. It seems, however, a good idea for our own writers to put their experiences and thoughts of the flowers into form, before all the wilderness and all our memory of the wilderness have disappeared.

BLUE LUPINE

"The earth is blue with them," wrote Thoreau of the lupines in Massachusetts. The Texas legislature chose it for the Texas state flower, making 'Texas blue bonnets' famous. But here, two thousand miles west of Thoreau's home and as many miles north of Texas, all the waste lands, the river bottoms, the railway embankments, ravines and alpine slopes are also 'blued' with them for several summer weeks. And far to the north on the bleak Barrens north of Slave Lake, the acres of land covered with lupine blue, in July, may be seen for miles.

These lupines are not, of course, all of the same variety, for there are some thirty species in Canada alone, but they are all so similar that they are easily recognised by the most amateur botanist.

The lupines of the Pacific coast are of many colours, but here on the eastern slope of the mountains they content themselves, for the most part, with blues and purples of varying intensities, though occasionally one comes across a magnificent pure white specimen. They range in size from low, dense clumps of deepest blue, found on open hillsides, to tall graceful spikes in the woodland glades which sometimes reach a height of four feet or more.

The roots of some species are edible, a Pacific coast variety being popularly known as Chinook liquorice. The seeds of the Mediterranean lupine were also used as food in the days of ancient Rome, where they were well boiled to remove the bitterness. Here lupine seeds are sometimes suspected of being poisonous though the plant itself is useful for grazing.

Few plants are so restless as the lupine, which provided a perfect subject for Darwin and other scientists in their study of the movement of plants. The leaves especially are continually on the move, the many long fingers opening and closing, or moving horizontally with every passing change of light and going quite obviously to sleep at the approach of nightfall. As subjects for scientific research they are ideal but as artists' models they are restless posers.

BLUE LUPINE

INDIAN PAINT BRUSH
Castilleja

As the black nave of an old cathedral is transformed to beauty by the splatter of light through the rich stained glasses of a master craftsman, so the brilliant scarlets and golds and blues of mountain flowers spread splashes of colour over the gloomy valleys. The red for this rich pattern is supplied for the most part by the scarlet bracts of the Indian Paint Brush. It is a familiar flower of the Yukon and was named by a Spanish botanist who found it in Central America.

INDIAN PAINT BRUSH

Here, in Old Man's Garden, we have every colour if not every species of Indian paint brush. There are yellows and creams, rich salmony-
pinks and whites as well as the most conspicuous vermilions. California
species grow in the open sun of the foothill slopes and the bright cold
magenta species, which is the only species met with in the Yukon, is
familiar on the edge of the timber line. Out on the lower slopes and
in the warm valleys it is usually a clear creamy pink and it chooses, for
its companions, the grey-blue lupines or the fluttering grey-green aspens. The vermilion species is usually found in the company of flowers
arrayed in the fullest intensity of primary colours—blue larkspur, yellow ragwort and golden gaillardia—and for background, the black-
green of the pines.

It is hard to believe that such a brilliantly coloured plant is on the
verge of being a parasite. It lives just within the law and so escapes the
punishment meted out to parasites. It possesses chlorophyll with which
to transform the minerals absorbed by its roots and so retains its green
leaves; but should temptation be placed in its way it is not above join-
ing its roots to the roots of other plants and stealing some of their already digested food.

The actual flower of the paint brush is of a pale greenish-yellow
colour, almost entirely wrapped in a long, tubular, greenish calyx. It is
the bracts that furnish the gaudy colour of the plant. Thoreau says, "It
is startling to see a leaf thus brilliantly painted, as if its tips were dipped
into some scarlet tincture, surpassing most flowers in intensity of
colour."

There is a delightful story of the origin of the paint brush told by
Mabel Burkholder in her book *Before the White Man Came*.

A young Indian maid fell in love with a wounded prisoner of her
tribe who was being nursed back to life only to be tortured later. She
planned his escape, and knowing that she would be punished for her
share in the plan, she went with him to his people. There they lived
happily until one day she was possessed of an overwhelming wave of
homesickness. She longed for just one glimpse of her people and their
camp.

At last she could bear it no longer but made her way back to the hill above her home. Hidden in the bushes, she heard passing riders discussing her and telling of the punishment that was her due for her traitorous action. Knowing she could never make her presence known to her people she decided to take back with her a drawing of her home. Cutting a gash in her foot, she dipped a twig in the blood and drew, on a piece of bark, a picture of the camp in the valley before her. Then, throwing the twig to the ground, she made her way back to her adopted home. Where the twig fell there grew up a little plant with a brush-like end, dyed with the blood which the girl had used for paint.

GERANIUM

Once the prophet Mohammed had occasion to wash his shirt on the bank of a stream. He laid it on some mallows to dry. They blushed with pleasure at being so honoured, and so became geraniums. Not, how-

GERANIUM

ever, the brilliant red and pink-flowered plants that we grow on our window sills. These are really pelargoniums from Africa.

The true geranium belongs to the woods of the northern hemisphere. The Greek name means crane and the common name of crane's bill, which is often used instead of geranium, was given it because of the long grooved beak of the pistil which is composed of five styles that adhere at the top.

The geranium best known in the west is the purple geranium (*Geranium carolinianum*) which attracted Palliser's attention as he approached the foothill regions of Alberta. It is a conspicuous plant of the early summer because of its rich, coarse foliage and the brilliant purple blooms, which it holds well aloft. It is much like the eastern species which is familiarly known as Herb Robert.

In autumn, when the flowers have gone, the plant once more claims attention because of the brilliance of its foliage reddened by the approach of winter.

A second variety, Richardson's geranium, is common in shadier situations, in open groves amongst the poplar trees. It shows a more delicate habit of growth, having thin leaves with slender, graceful stems which carry delicate white flowers.

TWIN FLOWER
Linnaea borealis

Karl von Linne, better known as Linnaeus, was one of the world's greatest naturalists. Born at Rashult, Sweden, he was for some years professor of natural history at the University of Upsala. Being the first naturalist to place the plants of the earth in a scientific classification according to the number of stamens and pistils, he has been called the father of modern botany.

Feeling that he would like at least one plant named for himself, he had his friend Dr. Gronovius propose the name of Linnaea for a delicately beautiful flower of the honeysuckle family which he had first fallen in love with while visiting Lapland, but which also grew in his own pine forests nearer home.

Linnaea is a woodland plant with creeping stems from which rise slender stalks, each bearing several pairs of round, evergreen leaves and two beautiful, drooping, bell-shaped flowers of pink or rose-tinted white. These small shy twin flowers were a wise choice to commemorate a great botanist for they are found, not only in the woods of Lapland and

TWIN FLOWER

Sweden, but through the north temperate zone the world around— on the steppes of Siberia, among the hills of Scotland and in the cool woods of North America, from Canada south to northern California. Trailing over moulding stumps and moss-covered rocks, the plant forms a dense mat of green leaves and tiny fragrant flowers, spreading a soft, springy carpet through the dim moist woods.

Little wonder that a botanist of the old world loved them and that a poet of the new world enshrined them in verse. Emerson writes:

He saw beneath dim aisles, in odorous beds
The slight Linnaea hang its twin-born heads
And blessed the monument of the man of flowers
Which breathes his sweet fame through the northern bowers.

MONESIS, PIPSISSEWA, and
WINTERGREEN

PYROLA

In the twilight of the under-forest, where a few long rays of light reach down to touch the cool moss carpet, several members of the heath family are at home. The best known of these is the red wintergreen or pyrola. Numerous rosy blossoms, nodding from an erect, reddish stalk, would m a k e i t conspicuous amongst a host of flowers. But in the eerie underworld, where only the thin stems and scanty foliage of the dwarf bilberry, the butterwort and the orchis dispute its right to the company of the pines, it is especially attractive. Deliciously fragrant and dainty, it reminds one of the lily of the valley from the garden.

The flower is as beautiful under close scrutiny as it is at the distance. The pale pink petals are shaded darker towards the edge; the calyx is deep red, as are also the tips of the stamens and the stigma which hangs well below the bell-shaped corolla. The leaves grow in a cluster at the base of the stem and are thick, tough and glossy. It is for these leaves that the plant is called wintergreen, for they are evergreen, retaining their colour through frost and snow. These leaves were also responsible for the very unlovely name of shin leaf by which this beautiful plant was known to our grandparents. The leaves were believed to have a healing effect on bruises and so were used for shin plasters.

There are several other wintergreens enough like the red one to be easily recognised. Chief among them are the green flowered wintergreen, which is slightly smaller and lacks the showy colour; and the one-sided wintergreen. In the latter the stems are weak enough to be bent gracefully downward by the weight of the blossoms which grow only on one side of the stem.

Closely related to the pyrola is the single beauty or single delight (*Monesis uniflora*), sometimes called one-flowered wintergreen. The single, nodding flower is so exquisitely designed that it is truly a delight, and one is surprised at the size of the flower on its tiny stem which seldom reaches more than four or five inches from the cluster of yellow-green leaves at the base. When the flower begins to fruit the stem gradually straightens so that the seed capsule is held erect.

With these flowers, or in a similar place, also grows the pipsissewa or prince's pine (*Chimaphila umbellata*). It is another member of the heath family with very decorative flowers. They are pinkish, but marked with a deep pink ring, growing in a spreading cluster. The bright shining evergreen leaves are very sharply toothed. They have been used in the manufacture of tonics.

ORCHIDS OF THE NORTH

The story of the orchid family is not necessarily a story of the tropics, though the present day craze for specimens of the tropical varieties almost equals the seventeenth century ardour for tulips—a passion that became known as tulipomania.

Orchids have advanced so far along the line of evolution that each species is adapted in size and shape to admit of fertilization by only one type of insect. In so adapting themselves they have developed many strange and striking forms of blossoms. One bears a flower that looks like a butterfly, another like a moth. An orchid found in Central America, near Panama, is called the dove plant or the Holy Spirit plant from its resemblance to the dove which symbolizes the Holy Ghost in religious paintings.

Common to the entire orchid family is a twist in the ovary of the flower by which what would otherwise be the upper petal, becomes the lower one. This lower lip is often grotesque in shape, frequently

CALYPSO, FLY-SPOTTED ORCHIS, HOODED LADIES'-TRESSES and YELLOW LADY'S SLIPPER

striking in colour, sometimes fringed or furrowed. In our northern temperate zone these strangely shaped flowers are all too small to attract much attention to themselves. Though they may quite truly be classed as orchids, they would not make much of a corsage for a great occasion. Amongst them are the pogonias, arethusas, grass-pinks, hellebores, ladies'-tresses, rattlesnake plantain and coral root.

The showiest of all our orchids, of course, is the yellow lady's slipper, with its pouch like an Ojibway moccasin. Its "golden slippers meet for fairies' feet" are found on mountain slopes close beside the glaciers and far out across the prairie.

The little daughter of an Indian chieftain, we are told in a poem by Ida F. Terry, gave her moccasins to a rabbit who had hurt his feet. It was a long way back to the Indian village and soon her own feet were torn and bleeding and she sank exhausted by the wooded pathway. The songbirds came to comfort her and while she slept they begged the Great Spirit to assist the little maiden. When she awoke, there before her, hanging on two slender stems, was a pair of dainty yellow moccasins, which she at once slipped on her bleeding feet. Inside the throat of the small lady's slipper, which seeks the shelter and seclusion of moist woods, may be seen the reddish purple spots and lines made by the bleeding of the maiden's wounded feet. The slippers had magic healing powers and she danced away through the forest.

Perhaps the magic healing powers were given the plant by poetic license, in order that the heroine might make the proper exit from the story, but in truth, the tubers of some varieties are dried and the nutritive starch appears on the market as a medicine.

In the mountains is found a rare white variety of the lady's-slipper, which may also have been magic slippers, for in the throat are spots and veinings of brightest red.

Calypso is a lovely little pink orchid which is often found in one's rambles through the woods. It is responsible for the only unscientific adjective in a botany of some nine hundred pages; the writer being betrayed by its charm into forsaking his science for a moment and describing it as a "beautiful little plant".

One can never forget the thrill of finding, for the first time, a clump of these tiny orchids while clambering over the sides of the mountains or in the deep still woods—the tall grandeur of the peaks or the impressive height of the great trees, and at one's feet the exquisite little calypso, with its spotted body and elfin wings tied with a silken cord to two round green leaves.

It was named in honour of the lovely nymph who lured Ulysses to forsake his wife for seven years — years which he spent living with Calypso on her lonely island.

As soon as the flower dies, the leaves are shed and are at once replaced with new ones that stay green all winter.

Also belonging to this same family are the rein orchis, the fly-spotted orchis and the hooded ladies'-tresses, the latter a pure white spike of the most fragrant flowers of the whole region, but often overlooked in the welter of mid-summer flowers. It is called ladies'-tresses because of the tight, perfect arrangement of the flowers on the stalk which remind one of a braid of hair.

The fly-spotted and rein orchis are often found in marshy spots sharing the warm air and cool root conditions with the pyrola and butterwort. Though a member of what is often considered a tropical family the fly-spotted orchis is found as far north as Fort Churchill on Hudson Bay.

THALICTRUM

There is a refinement and grace to plant life of the open woodlands which is lacking in plants that live in the full glare of the plain, and a sturdiness that does not belong to the plants of the deeper woods. Such an aristocrat is the meadow rue. Lacy, finely divided leaves cause it often to be mistaken for the dainty maiden hair fern in localities where that fern is not at home. But though elegant and feminine in appearance it is capable of lusty growth, reaching at times a height of six feet.

Its foliage alone is attractive enough to make it a popular and well known plant of every woodland but its blooms also are quaint and attractive. Belonging to a period far back in the evolutionary scale, it has not learned to depend on insects for cross-fertilization, but raises great feathery panicles of blossoms high above the surrounding vegetation so that the wind may carry its pollen abroad.

Nor is it sparing of pollen since it must depend on chance to carry it to its required destination. Neither male nor female flowers have petals and the small sepals drop early. The staminate flowers are a greenish-white while the feathery red-purple stigmas make doubly attractive the pistillate clusters.

THALICTRUM

GENTIAN

The gentian is a flower found throughout America and Europe. The species best known through poetry and prose is the fringed gentian.

Thou blossom! bright with autumn dew
And coloured with heaven's own blue
That openest when the quiet light
Succeeds the keen and frosty night.

Then doth thy sweet and quiet eye
Look through its fringes to the sky,
Blue, blue, as if the sky let fall
A flower from its cerulean wall.

William Cullen Bryant

Anything said of the blueness of the fringed gentian might be applied with equal aptness to the many varieties in our territory. They do not all, however, feel constrained to conform to the autumn blooming habits of the fringed gentian. They are to be found blooming practically throughout the summer.

GENTIAN

Some varieties are found only in the eastern part of Old Man's territory in Manitoba and Saskatchewan, North Dakota and eastern Montana. Others, somewhat smaller, cross the prairies to the mountains.

High in the mountains, amongst the towering cliffs and close pressing sky, grows a beautiful intense blue variety of breath-taking beauty. One finds it difficult to resist picking it in the hope of carrying home some of the magic, only to find that Emerson spoke truly when he said:

> I thought the sparrow's note from heaven,
> Singing at dawn in the alder bough.
> I brought him home in his nest at even,
> He sings the song, but it cheers not now,
> For I did not bring home the river and sky.

There is something in the rare air and the closeness of the sky that gives the alpine gentian's blue an intensity that belongs partly to the immense altitudes. It is really coloured with heaven's own blue. Removed from that blue the flower loses half its charm.

Gentians are not all open, skyward looking flowers. In many varieties the corolla opens only slightly to the warm rays of the mid-day sun but closes hurriedly at the first approach of evening, giving rise to the well known child's story of the selfish flower who would not open its petals to shelter the fairy and so was doomed always to remain closed, and the good flower who was rewarded with a fringe and the beauty of the skies.

Though celebrated in poetry the fringed gentian has not eclipsed entirely the beautiful varieties which do not open wide fringed eyes to the sky but peep shyly from closed or half-closed lids.

> Beside the brook and on the umbered meadow,
> Where yellow fern-tufts fleck the faded ground
> With folded lids beneath their palmy shadow
> The Gentian nods in dewy slumber bound.

The flower got its name from Gentius, the king of Illyria, who, according to Pliny, first discovered its medicinal properties. This probably refers to the common yellow gentian of the Alps and Pyrenees. The peasants gather the bitter roots of this species and sell it for flavouring bitters and for use as a tonic and in diseases of the digestive system. Large quantities of this root are imported into the United States and Canada.

GAILLARDIA

Gaillardia aristata

Of all the flowers of the west, gaillardia has made itself most at home in the gardens of the world. Its bright yellow rays and rich red centres early attracted the attention of the botanist and gardener; and the ease with which it is transferred to the garden must have contributed to its popularity. Its long tap roots make it difficult to transplant, but the seeds are easily gathered on the prairie and grow in the garden with very little care, giving a gorgeous blaze of colour by the second year. Not only are the flowers themselves a brilliant spot of colour but the seeds are loved by the goldfinches whose visits to the garden are continuous from the time the first blossoms open until long after the last ones have vanished.

Perhaps Frederick Pursh was the first to bring it into the civilization of the garden when he was in charge of the large Botanic Garden

GAILLARDIA

in New York, early in the nineteenth century. To him, at least, goes the credit for the first description and naming of the plant.

That florists were still absorbingly interested in the plant a century later is evidenced by this story told by Edna Kells, of the great Luther Burbank, famous experimenter in the improvement and cross-fertilization of plants.

> "On one occasion when he was travelling across the continent he was observing as closely as possible the flowers and plants of the prairie. When the train stopped, he got off and walked away a short distance searching for plants. So absorbed was he in the search that he failed to notice the warning whistle. The train pulled out and was some distance on its way before the conductor discovered that his distinguished passenger was missing. There was a commotion among the crew and much wiring back and forth when the next station was reached. Eventually the difficulty was straightened out and Burbank continued his journey. Railway officials were profuse in their apologies, but so far as their passenger was concerned apologies were unnecessary. " 'It really doesn't matter,' he said, 'I've got my gaillardia.' "

Nurserymen are still interested in experimenting with the gaillardia, and one of their most recent presentations to the world of amateur gardeners is a double gaillardia.

Its specific name, *aristata,* means that the scales of the pappus are aristate or tipped with an awn or bristle. The emphasis on such an inconspicuous part of such a showy flower may be explained by the fact that Pursh named it from a dried specimen and had no way of knowing how unusually beautiful it is in its natural state.

BINDWEED
Convolvulus

The bindweed has made itself so completely at home in this, its adopted country, that it cannot be ignored in any book on flowers, whether of the garden or the wilds.

In a book on garden flowers it is classed as one of the worst of noxious weeds. There is a theory that it is fertilized by only one kind of moth, the *Sphinx convolvuli,* and that in places, such as Scotland, where the moth is lacking, the *convolvulus* is seldom found wild. The plant has insured itself against extinction, however, by having long running rootstocks, any small section of which will produce a plant. It is therefore very difficult to eradicate.

BINDWEED

Rapin must have been a gardener for he had a very low opinion of the plant.

> Convolvulus will next in boundless store
> Cloath the moist vale with yet unfinished Flowers
> These rude Essays were first for lilly's meant
> When Nature, on a nobler work intent,
> First took the pencil and began to paint.

No one need be told that this plant with the large, fragile looking, trumpet-shaped flower belongs to the morning glory family. Even the most casual observer would instinctively apply the popular name of wild morning glory.

In contrast to the gardener, the writer of a book on wild flowers, who is free to consider the plant as a purely aesthetic expression on the part of the Creator might easily describe it in Celia Thaxter's words—

> The bindwood's ivory buds that glow
> As delicately blushing as a shell.

and feel with Thoreau when he says, "The convolvulus is at its best now. It always refreshes me to see it. I associate it with the holiest morning hours. It may preside over my morning walk and thoughts."

In one way the bindweed is a curiosity in the plant world, for both the pollen and pistil are white instead of the customary yellow. It is also an exceedingly rapid climber. Turning counter-clockwise, it describes a complete circle in just two hours.

MILKWEED

> In dusky pods the milkweed
> Its hidden silk has spun.

Milkweed is beloved of poets because of its handsome pods which pop open along one side and pour forth a cloud of silken-haired seeds to float off on the mountain breeze. But from the standpoint of design it is the flower that is interesting. With its dark red turned-back petals, its high crown with exquisitely modelled hoods, its incurved horns and the ingenious arrangement for compelling insects to work for it, it is not only a triumph in executive ability but in decorative design also.

But not only to the mind of the artist and poet does the milkweed appeal. It is also beloved of the scientist. No other plant, except the strangely over-developed orchid and the gruesome little carnivorous plants, has received as much attention from scientists as the milkweed. The scientific account reads like a modern horror and crime story with a beautiful friendship to add enrichment. One may read pages of scientific detail on how the milkweed traps small insects, hanging them by the tongue until they die a frightful death because they tried to steal the nectar made for larger insects; how the milky juice repels the visits of marauding ants and small crawling bugs, coating their feet as they climb the stalk and eventually crippling them by hardening so they cannot remove it; and most interesting of all, the relationship between the milkweeds and the monarch butterflies, those beautiful orange and black butterflies so common in our gardens, which are always found hovering about a clump of milkweed. How far along the road of evolution has this highly organized flower travelled from those first simple flowers which produced their pollen in such amazing quantities that they could trust an erratic breeze to carry it to its destination! The mon-

MILKWEED

arch butterfly has a tongue perfectly adapted to the needs of the milk-weed and so does the work of fertilization for it. In return, the milk-weed's leaves nourish the grubs of the butterfly and its acrid juice is so distasteful to birds that both grub and butterfly are immune from the attacks that so diminish the grubs of other species.

Moths and butterflies, those ethereal beauties who should thrive on sunlight and nectar are, alas for our sense of fitness, quickly attracted by a vile and putrid odour. Since all the flower's efforts are to attract these butterflies, the milkweed's fragrance enters into neither poetry nor art.

To those who are not scientifically, artistically nor poetically inclined, perhaps the plant's more practical aspects will appeal. The Indians made rope of its tough fibre and there have been recent attempts to use its milky juice for the making of rubber.

FORGET-ME-NOT
Myosotis

This beautiful little plant has had a place in the hearts of men since the dawn of history. Some of the sweetest lines of English poetry do it honour. The name of the plant is the same in many languages and wherever it grows it is the symbol of modesty, constancy and innocence —all that is most noble.

Most of the true forget-me-nots or *Myosotis* (the Greek word means mouse ear) found in America belong to an immigrant family from Europe which has made itself at home along the banks of eastern streams. There is, however, a native variety of the true forget-me-not found at high altitudes. It is about four to six inches high. Its tiny turquoise flowers are very fragrant and its nutlets quite smooth.

A beautiful, showy plant with the same constant blue eyes as the forget-me-not is, in this country, often confused with it. This is *Lap-*

pula floribunda or false forget-me-not, easily distinguished from the *Myosotis* because of its seeds. These are very sticky burrs for which the plant is sometimes known as stick seed. A pale, rather insignificant plant at lower levels, the cool moist air of the upper slopes produces a larger flower of a more intense blue so that many people consider it a purely mountain flower. What matter if it be a noxious weed in the heat and drought of the prairie? In the rarer air it is both beautiful and fragrant—one of the beauties of the alpine slopes and pool's edges, worthy of all the noble sentiments that come to it from its namesake of the old world.

FORGET-ME-NOT

THE PINK FAMILY

The Pink family is widely distributed over the world, belonging mostly, however, to the temperate and cold climates. It derives its name from the word pinken, to scallop. These flowers borrowed their name from a verb and then gave it to a colour. The colour pink comes from the flower just as the colour orange comes from the fruit.

The pink family contains several beautiful flowers such as the innumerable varieties of carnations, but other members might be classed as hoboes. The *Silene* or catchfly, the *Cerastium* or chickweed and the *Lychnis* or cockle have received much attention in the weed books.

Bladder campion (*Silene vulgaris*) comes to us from Europe. It is often met with at the roadsides and in fields and may be easily recognised by its curious inflated calyx. This is the 'bladder' of the flower's name, and this characteristic also explains why it is sometimes called 'cow-bell' in Canada, and in England 'white bottle'. The calyx is further remarkable for its exquisite veining.

Silene was named for Silenus, a god of Bacchus' train, whom the Greeks represented as an old gentleman in a highly intoxicated condition.

Many of the species are quite viscid, hence the other common name of catchfly. The plant uses its sticky juice as a defence against small insects which attempt to steal its nectar without paying for it by carrying pollen.

When Minerva lived on earth she had for pets a score of owls that lived on flies. She used to send a little boy named Campion to entrap

Moss Campion and Bladder Campion

the insects, and in the morning he would set forth, carrying a big bladder bag in which to place his captives. Campion used to seek the shadiest corner and sleep throughout the stillness of the day, his bladder bag lying empty by his side. Days passed and the owls languished and grew thinner. Finally Minerva turned Campion into a flower as punishment, and to this day we see him with the bladder wherein he was supposed to keep the flies while wandering in the sunshine. And still his head droops with shame by night when the hooting of the owls reminds him of his laziness.

The catchflies and cockles are so well known across the prairies and high into the mountains that little more need be said of them. But one form of *Silene* (*S. acaulis*) deserves special mention. Moss campion or moss pink, as it is called, is a dwarf arctic-alpine plant that is fed by a deep root. It has tiny leaves, which are very numerous, narrow and pointed. Its showy masses of bright pink flowers, which grow in tufts from six to twenty inches in diameter, are not easily overlooked by those who brave the rocky slopes above the timberline. Since it adds colour and beauty to rocky surfaces from 6,000 to 10,000 feet above sea level, it avoids the weed books and restores the family to a position of respect.

From the brilliant beauty of the moss pink it seems a sudden drop back to the mundane chickweed. It also is a member of the pink family. The worst offender, however, is the imported chickweed which is so troublesome in the garden. The native varieties are much more showy and less tenacious. All have white flowers. The five snow white petals with the toothed edge of the field-mouse-eared chickweed have won for it the title of 'Star of Bethlehem' which no one begrudges it. In fact, in the west the plant is sometimes cultivated for its beauty.

There is an alpine mouse-eared chickweed with whitish leaves and large white flowers. Dr. Sutherland, who went to Baffin Bay in 1851 to search for Sir John Franklin, found it growing close to the icebergs. He remarked that Button Point looked as green as any English meadow. The foxtail grass and chickweed (*Cerastium alpinum*) and hosts of other grasses and herbaceous plants grew among the bones of animals and the filth of the Eskimo habitations to "a degree of luxuriance which no one would be willing to assign to the 73rd degree of north latitude."

THISTLE

The thistle is another of those plants over which there is a continual difference of opinion, some considering only its weed-like characteristics and others finding great pleasure in it from an aesthetic point of view. Certainly we have been trained by designers to see great decorative qualities in its shapely leaves and compact flower heads, and by weed books to see danger in its fast-spreading seeds and roots.

When the Danes invaded Scotland they stole silently, by night, upon the Scottish camp, concealing the tread of marching feet by going barefoot. But a Dane stepped on a thistle and his startled exclamation revealed the presence of the invaders. No wonder the flower was elevated in rank from a wayside flower to a national institution.

Except where farmers are concerned, the aura of symbolism it bears as the national flower of Scotland easily out-balances the poor name given it as a noxious weed. "Noble and kindly within, it is resolute to withstand aggression from without." There is a delightful touch of humour in the motto the Scot affixes to the flower, "No one touches me with impunity", or "Wha daur meddle wi' me".

THISTLE

The Order of the Thistle was instituted by James VII of Scotland, James II of England. The motto is centred around the emblem which, before the seventeenth century, was the badge of the House of Stuart. The collar of the Order of the Thistle is of gold, of most beautiful workmanship, with the two ancient symbols of the Picts and Scots interlaced throughout the exquisite design—the thistle and the sprigs of rue.

Several kinds of thistle are commonly known here. The prairie thistle or western bull thistle is a handsome, native perennial that grows from one to three feet high and carries large flower-heads of rich reddish purple. It is called wavy-leaved thistle (*Carduus undulatus*) because of the large, long leaves with wavy margins, triangularly lobed and sharply toothed. It is listed as a weed but is easily controlled.

The most commonly seen thistle is known here as the Canada or field thistle, but it is really the creeping thistle of the old world which has been introduced into almost all the newer countries and has proved a troublesome enemy of field crops.

Travellers to the mountains will not fail to notice the tall white thistle, conspicuous because of its size, which makes even the handsome wavy-leaved thistle seem small. The leaves of this thistle are very spiny or, as Julia Henshaw says, cobweb-woolly. In favourable locations it grows to a height of four feet and is left severely alone by the flower-picking traveller.

WAYBRED

Plantago lanceolata

There is, along our roadsides, an insignificant little weed which, if noticed at all, is usually dismissed with a wave of the hand, as an undesirable immigrant. "Oh, that is just a weed from Europe", we say. But that little weed could tell a story as exciting as any tale of travel and adventure in the world today.

Its story begins long ago in the days when all men were Handsome Knights in Armour and all women were Beautiful Damosels or Ladies in Distress. One of these Handsome Knights married a Beautiful Damosel and, true to the customs of the time, unclasping his hands from their first embrace, he went off to battle. "Watch here", he said lightly, as he left her there by the roadside, "and you will soon see me riding back to you."

The Beautiful Damosel at once became a Lady in Distress. By the side of the road she waited while loving attendants brought her food and waited on her with anxious hearts.

Her beauty faded.

By the side of the road she pined and drooped and wilted and finally became a humble little wayside flower that still refused to forsake her watch. The people of the countryside, descendants perhaps of her loving attendants, named her waybret or waybred and regarded her with patient amusement.

Then she went to wait by other roadsides. She began to follow Englishmen on their travels here and there, always hoping that sometime, somewhere, she would see her lost lover riding down the road to her.

When she followed the Englishman to America, keeping eagerly just a little ahead of his footsteps into the wilderness, her name was changed again. She now became known as Englishman's foot.

Hiawatha saw her and told his people of the men whom Iagoo had already seen—people with white painted faces and hair on their chins.

> I have seen it in a vision
> Seen the great canoe with pinions
> Seen the people with white faces
> People of the wooden vessels
> From the regions of the morning
> Whereso'er they move, before them
> Springs a flower unknown among us
> Springs the White Man's Foot in blossom.

Some time when you have an hour or two to spare sit down beside her on the roadside and let her tell you of the drama she has seen, passing her by on the roadways of the world. It will be an hour well spent.

This plant is now commonly known as plantain (*Plantago lanceolata*) and is listed in the weed books together with the common plantain (*P. major*), a native of this continent, which is broader-leaved with flowers in longer spikes.

CONE-FLOWER

Lepachys columnifera

If autumn is a season of gold, the prairie summer is too. When the blue distances are shut out by the smoke of the forest fires and the

Cone-Flower

trees of the river valleys are shimmering lines of heat waves in the distance, the prairie world is a world of gold—bright gold of sunshine, pale gold of ripening oat fields, red gold of wheat, dull gold of the ripened prairie grass and, above all, the clear yellow gold of summer flowers, gaillardia with their rich red centres, sunflowers, ragwort and golden-rod.

The most ornamental of all these flowers of the hot sunshine is the cone-flower. It is even more decorative than the thistle but has not yet become well enough known to compete with it. With its long drooping rays and purple-black cylindrical centre, a cluster of these flowers is like a troupe of gold dust twins, with stiffly starched yellow skirts outspread, and little black bodies, ready to step into a summertime masque. The familiar name of niggerhead is obviously suitable, the marvel being that it came to the western flower from a closely related but much smaller-centred eastern species.

The drooping rays are at times streaked with vermilion, or more rarely are that delightful reddish-puce colour so popular in wallflowers. These reddish flowers have been given the very suitable specific name of *pulcherrima*.

Like all the sunflower family, the cluster or head of flowers resembles a single flower. The unobservant take the rays for petals and the disc flowers for stamen and pistil.

The cone-flower is a distinctly prairie flower, disappearing entirely at the approach of the foothills or the brush country of the northern areas.

MONKEY FLOWER

Mimulus

In Europe when Linnaeus was first bringing order out of the chaos of what passed as botany in those days, a dull insignificant little plant, which was supposed to be a cure for scrofula, emerged from the disorder and was placed in a genus named *Scrophulariaceae*. Later, America proved to be the home of many members of this particular family and

some of the most beautiful wild flowers of the world inherited its repell-
ant name.

As one turns the pages of the botany through the section devoted to
this family one feels that this must be the zoo of plant society. Not only
is it a very handsome family but also a very odd and original one, as
indicated by the popular names of its members. Here are a few—
monkey flower, toadflax, snapdragon, fox-glove, turtlehead, beard-
tongue, owl's clover, elephant head, Indian warrior, duck bill, Indian paintbrush, blue-eyed Mary and kitten tails.

The monkey flowers turn laughing faces to the traveller in higher

MIMULUS

altitudes, from the mossy borders of many an alpine stream. They are
very human little things and, like the pansy, seem to turn real faces
to the passerby. For this reason they were given the name of *mimulus*
or little mimic.

The red *mimulus* is an extremely handsome plant which hangs from
a rock over the dark edge of a deep glacial lake or covers the small
grassy island of a lagging stream, sun-warmed and drousy. In these
favoured spots, sheltered by other moisture-loving plants, it attains a
height of one and a half or two feet. Each blossom has a long green
calyx, from which protrudes a richly coloured tube that spreads out into
two lips, the upper one two-lobed, the lower one three-lobed and spreading. The colour is a glowing purplish red.

Captain Lewis first found it as he passed near Glacier Park in the year 1805 and so this handsome variety is known as *Mimulus lewisii*.

The yellow *mimulus* is even quainter and seems more like a little clown than the red. Its fat blossoms seem top heavy on the slender stem and the bright yellow is mottled and pencilled with red. It is even more fond of moisture than the larger variety and nestles in mossy beds that are kept marshy by melting snow or the cold water of hidden streams oozing through the rocks.

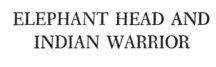

ELEPHANT HEAD AND INDIAN WARRIOR

This queer *Scrophulariaceae* family carries its amazing tradition further in the naming of one of the strangest groups of flowers of the region, the *pedicularis*. *Pediculus* is the Latin word for louse. In English the plant is known as lousewort because, as the writings of old herbalists explain, it is a plant which "filled sheep and other cattle that feed in the meadows where it groweth, full of lice".

In our territory we have three varieties of *pediularis*. Perhaps the most interesting is the one which, from its specific name, must have been reported from Greenland, *Pedicularis groenlandica*. If the tiny reddish flowers are examined closely they will be found to resemble an elephant's head, the long beak of the

ELEPHANT HEAD and
CONTORTED LOUSEWORT

corolla being upcurved like an elephant's trunk, the drooping lobes of the corolla resembling ears. So uncanny is the likeness that it requires no imagination to see the elephant's head and the flower could have had no other name.

The name of Indian warrior for *Pedicularis bracteosa* is not so easily explained. Since this is the famous wood betony which has cured so many of the ills of the world it is mentioned in more detail under medicinal plants.

The greatest unpoetic injustice of the world of plants has been directed against a conspicuous plant of the meadows above the timberline, where any flower becomes one of God's miracles. It has cream coloured, beaked flowers set in a cluster at the top of the stalks and is found growing in clumps in alpine meadows and on rocky slopes. When one waxes poetic about its beauty under the threatening cliffs it is well to remember that its name, translated, means 'contorted lousewort'.

BEARD-TONGUE
Pentstemon

Of all the flowers brought to me for identification, the beard-tongues are the commonest. The average person longs for a simple name, as easily remembered as blue beard-tongue (and the hyphen is usually misplaced); but the average person is apt to doubt one's sincerity or knowledge if the name is applied too often. Yet beard-tongue is a name coined to replace the Greek name of *Pentstemon* which designated an entire tribe; so the name beard-tongue is really correct for about two hundred varieties. Perhaps it is fortunate that not more than twenty-five or thirty of them grow in our territory, so the authors of popular names have some hope of covering them all some day.

The finding of the sub-genus *Pentstemon* is accredited to John

Mitchell, who was one of those very earliest of North American flower enthusiasts. He died in Virginia about the year 1772. Amongst his collection of new world flowers was a solitary eastern specimen of a member of the figwort family which had five stamens. This was a rare and interesting find, because all known members of this family had hitherto possessed either two or four stamens. A new sub-genus was created for this specimen and was called *Pentstemon,* that is 'five stamens'.

From that time on every expedition that went westward brought home new specimens. The purple flowered *Pentstemon menziesii* was discovered by Menzies at Nootka Sound. Douglas collected some twenty of them. Nuttall, Fremont and others came home with their herbaria crowded. More recently, collectors like Rydberg have rounded out our knowledge of the group in prairie and mountain regions where it is

PENTSTEMON FRUTICOSA, ACUMINATUS, and CONFERTUS

represented even more numerously than on the coast, until now there are the two hundred named species already mentioned.

Of the five stamens which give this group its name, the fifth is usually sterile and more or less bearded, which explains the name beard-tongue. They range in colour from white to yellow, rose, purple and darkest ultramarine. There are also many sizes, but all possess a tubular blossom with two lips, the lower of which is heavily bearded.

On the cut-banks of the prairie, on dry gravel heaps, or on railway embankments, one of the most beautiful of the tribe is found blooming in June. The Indians called it fire-taste and used it for a medicine, as a pain-killer, long before it was first found and officially recorded by David Douglas, who was responsible for naming all of our most familiar varieties. He must have been running short of names when he called it *Pentstemon acuminatus* because of the rather inconspicuous point on the tip of the leaves which causes botanists to describe the leaves as acuminate.

P. acuminatus is one of those plants which has adapted itself to dry situations by developing a whitish bloom on its smooth stems and leaves. This gives the whole plant, when not in bloom, a greyish appearance. The stems are quite pink, with a shading of yellow-green, the bracts which support the flowers are reddish-green. The buds form a dark blue sphere coiled on a red-purple tube and when the flower opens the lips are brilliant azure blue while the tube still retains its pink. This mixture of colours gives a lovely irridescent quality to the spike, which grows to a height of ten to twenty inches.

P. fruticosa, a shrubby plant, was also found by David Douglas, who is responsible for naming more than a dozen species. Its showy purple and pink flowers form mats of colour on hillsides and mountain sides and cover the rocky beds of mountain streams.

Sometimes the seeds of this showy *Pentstemon* ride down to the prairies on the waters of an unusually full spring freshet and, weather conditions being suitable, the river bottoms of the prairie burst, next spring, into unexpected blossom. Drought proves too much for consistent growth, however, and they retire once more to their mountains.

These plants make ideal additions to the prairie garden where they can be encouraged with a little more water than nature supplies. They stand the heat well and, being perennial, come up in the same place year after year, or replant themselves in sufficient quantities without overrunning the rest of the garden.

There is also a white species, *P. albus,* much more woolly than the foregoing, which thrives on the dry prairies.

P. procerus and *P. confertus* are common, both in the mountains and in moist meadows across the prairie. The first is a very rich, dark blue, and the other a pale creamy yellow. The blooms of these are much smaller, but they make up in numbers what they lack in size, growing in tight clusters round tall stiff stems of from one to two feet.

As John Macoun came westward, botanizing, in 1872, he was impressed by the *Pentstemon* shortly after leaving Winnipeg.

"The prairies we have been passing through in Manitoba were then called the weedy prairies on account of the number of tall flowering plants that grew upon them. Before us, while we stayed at Rat Creek, extended a flat plain, twelve miles wide without a house, and one unbroken mass of tall flowering plants; pentstemon, sunflowers, goldenrods, asters. In the next 150 miles we passed through a beautiful country and to us Easteners it looked as if it were a perfect garden."

ROCK BREAKERS
Saxifrage

Man, with his little life and his tremendous hurry, has no time to consider the beauty of his tools. But Old Man, with centuries, even aeons, at his disposal, has chosen his with cunning and sensitive care.

His pruning-knives that cut and trim are the ivory teeth of the deer and the antelope. The pests that threaten the health of the woods are searched out and destroyed by the sharp eyes and sharper beaks of the many coloured birds. The planting and watering is left to the rains and the winds. But perhaps the most charming of all his tools are the ones Old Man has chosen for his rock breakers. He seems to have taken a whimsical delight in giving the heaviest task to the most fragile of tools.

The *saxifrages* or rock breakers (from *saxum*—rock and *frango*—I break), rooted in the clefts of perpendicular crags or slopes of rocky debris, are the daintiest of flowers. But in spite of their apparent fragility, their home is in the north temperate zone where they prefer a high altitude.

The mitreworts, tellima and tiarella are all members of the *saxifrage* family who owe their fame to the profusion of their coarse, richly green foliage. The mitrewort is one of the few really green flowers of the region. The small petals are divided into short thread-like lobes so that the blossom looks like a tiny spider's web rather than a flower with petals and all the other flower organs.

Tellima is even more prolific than the mitrewort. It is easily recognised by the numerous round cream-coloured or green blossoms set close against long slender stalks which rise well above the great quantities of foliage. The leaves are large, rounded and lobed, with fine white hairs standing up all over them.

Saxifrage

The commonest of the little rockbreakers of our district is the foam-flower or Nancy-over-the-ground. It is sometimes called tiarella or lace flower. It is a conspicuous plant along trails through the heavy woods where it makes a low creeping hedge of handsome dark green leaves over which is spread a veil of foam-like flowers.

The species already mentioned are common across the continent, but in the upper mountain regions there are strange and beautiful varieties of many colours. Watered by the spray from dripping rocks and cooled by winds from year round snow, they thrive in cracks and bits of mould on the face of cliffs. Wherever one goes through the mountains, from the timber-line to the open rocky places at lower altitudes, one is sure to find some member of this family.

TELLIMA, TIARELLA and MITREWORT

WILD ROSE

Let us not search, as men have done since Chaucer's day, for adjectives to describe the rose. The rose has turned the tables on the poets by becoming, itself, a description. A man may say glibly "O my love's like a red, red rose." But it is another thing to say what the red, red rose is like. Roses are . . . roses. It takes a man of the rare gifts of Thomas Moore to say:

> Rose thou art the sweetest flower
> That ever drank the amber shower.
> Rose thou art the fondest child
> Of dimpled Spring, the wood nymph wild.

The agricultural departments of the western provinces, be it noted, are not hampered by vain seeking after words. "Roses", they say, "are weeds. Eradication: plough fairly deep using a sharp share. Cultivate thoroughly throughout the season with a springtooth cultivator."

WILD ROSE

Roses are as common as that in the west—as common as the sun, the blue skies and the summer breeze.

To Daniel Harmon of the North West Company, the rose was neither a weed nor the "fondest child of dimpled Spring". It was a grim necessity. He writes in January, 1804:

> "I have come here to Lac la Pèche, to pass the winter by the side of the X. Y. people.* For some time after our arrival we subsisted on rose buds, a kind of food neither very palatable nor very nourishing, which we gathered in the fields. They were better than nothing since they would just support life."

Had Daniel Harmon been able to read recent medical reports he would surely have been comforted by the fact that his food was amazingly rich in vitamin content.

To find a suitable floral emblem for a province that includes within its boundaries every sort of land from swamp to desert, from highest mountain peaks to broadest prairie, is no small problem, but the province of Alberta has solved it by choosing the wild rose, which is at home in any surroundings.

Several species of rose are to be found in our western area, distinguished mainly by some peculiarity of stem or berry. Nothing could be more beautiful than the pink roses that clamber up the river banks in June, except perhaps the large prairie roses, ranging from white to almost red, which cover the open prairies in July and remain in bloom until late August.

It seems very suitable that Monsieur Bourgeau, the naturalist who accompanied Captain Palliser on his explorations of the west and who collected so many of the prairie plants for European herbaria, should have been honoured by having his name given to one of the wild roses of the new country. A low-growing inhabitant of the woods, which has rose-coloured blossoms and stems densely covered with weak bristles, has been called *Rosa bourgeauiana*.

---

*The 'X. Y. people' were rival fur traders who afterwards joined forces with the North West Company.

PHACELIA

According to Saunders the first phacelia was found by a naturalist friend of Linnaeus at the extreme lower tip of South America. For twenty years it puzzled botanists who placed it first in one genus, then in another, until finally they settled the problem by creating a new genus. The word phacelia was based on the Greek word for cluster, and was suggested by the crowded flowers. Since the first discovery, more than one hundred species have been found, all natives of the western hemisphere and most of them of western North America.

PHACELIA

A handsome variety with rich purple-blue flowers clustered in long spike-like panicles and with downy, deeply-cleft foliage is often found on dry open hillsides in the foothill regions between plain and mountain. The territory covered by this striking flower includes Montana and southern Alberta, north to the Bow and into Crowsnest Pass. A similar species climbs on into the higher mountains and is common above the timber-line. There is also a white variety common nearly everywhere in the foothills region, ranging from plains to highest alpine rock slides. In this species the leaves are not toothed; they are lance-shaped and densely covered with fine, stiff grey hairs. The flowers are white, but against the dull grey of the foliage look rather dirty and are not especially attractive. The plant at times forms large clumps and is often conspicuous, but is not attractive enough to claim much attention.

ALPINE POPPY

Papaver pygmaeum

Many flower lovers will cover the country thoroughly year after year without ever seeing the alpine poppy. Yet it is worthy of mention be-

ALPINE POPPY

cause it is so rare and because it is the only relative in this part of the world of the showy Iceland poppy which has made itself so completely at home at Banff and Lake Louise. The alpine poppy is such a pale, insignificant plant that only a flower lover would notice it. You are not likely to come across it in the flowering meadows but rather on exposed rock slides where other vegetation is scant.

The flower, borne on a slender stem, varies in colour from yellow to reddish-orange. It is formed like the common poppy but has only four petals. All the leaves are in a tuft at the base of the plant. In a report by Macoun and Holm of the botany of a Canadian arctic expedition, the alpine poppy is mentioned as illustrating the theory that similar flower species can be developed in two entirely separate parts of the world if conditions are similar. Specimens of the alpine poppy were found in South Kootenay Pass, Waterton Lakes and near Stanton Lake (altitude 7,500 feet). James Macoun sent samples to the British Museum and was informed that they were the first record from this continent of a species which had already been found in the Pyrenees.

The report goes on to point out that the finding of a flower in the Rockies that has hitherto been found only in the Pyrenees does not necessarily mean that the continents were once one.

> "It would certainly seem too strange, I think, to explain the presence of this south European species in the Rocky Mountains as being in any way connected with some centre in the Pyrenees. When a small genus has actually been produced at stations so remote from each other, but in the Alpine regions, there seems to be a corresponding probability to suppose that the same species might also be produced independently from more than a single centre, so long as the conditions are the same, in respect to climate and soil and in regard to association with allied types."

If you are curious enough to want to check on this rare little plant, try looking for it at Sexton Glacier and Piegan Pass in Glacier Park, or about the Carthew Lakes in Waterton National Park.

A SILVER INDICATOR

Eriogonum

Eriogonums, which are of the same family as the rhubarb, are distinctly western, being for the most part occupants of open rocky slopes, arid plains, mountain prairies and bad lands. They are curious little flowers, making themselves conspicuous by the grouping of myriads of tiny flowers into handsome, flat-topped clusters, with a whorl of narrow leaves at the top of the main stem, where it divides into smaller stems, to support the flower umbels. The leaves, usually silvery, are clustered close to the ground. The flowers are white or yellow, but with age become red-tinged until they could be more nearly described as red.

One of the commonest of northern species is *Eriogonum ovalifolium*. It has leaves like grey-green felt and flowers of creamy-yellow tipped with red. In the early days of the west, when prospecting was carried on by guess and superstition rather than by science, when enthusiastic explorers reported gold amongst the grass roots, and gems by the shores of every mountain lake, this species was the centre of fame's fickle spotlight. Because of its silvery leaves it was supposed that its roots fed on silver ore and the plant probably paid for its fame with its life. In those days, with several other closely related species, it was known as silver plant.

But if men were disappointed in their search for silver at its roots, swarms of honey bees found in its flowers something more precious than silver. As the honey bee escaped from domesticity in the east, it moved westward across the continent far in

ERIOGONUM

advance of the human swarms. It found, in the far west, flowers so generous with their nectar that they have since been used for the production of honey on a commercial scale and the eriogonum has become known as the bee plant.

E. *umbellatum* is a common mountain species of a creamy-yellow colour which turns purplish-rose with age. Its tall umbrella-like umbels have given it the common name of umbrella plant. This plant is found farther north than the handsome sulphur plant (*E. flavum*), the beautiful clear yellow eriogonum which colours the slopes of Waterton and Glacier Parks early in July and which is found as far east as Manitoba.

Amongst approximately 125 species, there are varieties suited to conditions from the Manitoba plains to the highest mountains. *E. androsaceum* is a densely silvery little plant which forms mats of rounded leaves in high passes and summits to a height of 8,000 feet. Such a handsome and unusual flower could not be long ignored by garden lovers and has become a favourite for rock garden culture.

FLOWERS OF THE MOON
Mentzelia decapetala

One of the most beautiful of the summertime memories of old timers of the prairie is the walk, out in the white moonlight, along the edge of the cut-bank to see the moonflower or midnight lily in blossom—that creamy exotic flower, that holds in its petals all the elusive wonder of the white night itself. At the approach of darkness, it opens its immaculate petals wide to the moonlight, its centre a great bristling mass of pale yellow stamens. Even the youngest children were allowed to sit up late one night each summer for a glimpse of its beauty; for in daytime it is but a shrivelled mass of brown petals and dusty sharp-pointed leaves.

Of course its name is not really moonflower. The early settlers seemed doomed to give the wrong name to flowers, because they often chose names from unrelated but similar flowers of the old country. The name given in the botanies to this ethereal flower of the prairie moonlight is *Mentzelia decapetala*. The common names are prairie lily and stick leaf.

The California relatives of this flower are called *buena muter* (good woman) by the Spanish population because they stick to man with constancy. Its shiny brittle leaves are supplied with bristling points like thistle leaves.

In other species the five creamy white-pointed petals surrounding the bristling yellow stamens have given rise to the name of blazing star. In our prairie variety it is interesting to note that the petals are accompanied by five sepals of the same waxy whiteness, so that the flower has the appearance of a ten-petalled (*decapetala*) flower.

MENTZELIA DECAPETALA

SAND LILY

Pachylophus caespitosus

Another beautiful night-blooming plant of the prairie is known by the common names of sand lily and alkali lily. It is closely allied to the evening primrose and so is at times called tufted primrose. It is a low-growing plant covered with large, four-petalled flowers. These are a beautiful, pure white when the flower opens, but as soon as the sun touches them they turn to glowing pink, and finally become red and wilted by noon.

The large, showy petals suggest the ears of an elephant and so it was given the scientific name of *Pachylophus*. The *caespitosus* refers to

SAND LILY

its habit of producing tufts of leaves along a thick, decumbent stem. The Blackfeet also took the size of the petals into account, their name for it being 'wide leaves'. They used it in their medicines for relieving inflammation and reducing swellings.

The sand lily grows in alkali soils and gravel beds, or on the clay banks of rivers in the driest parts of the prairie. Prairie gardeners count it as one of their special treasures. It is a showy, decorative plant, which grows easily year after year, and is covered with a mass of beautiful blooms from mid-June until frost.

DRUMMOND'S DRYAS
Dryas drummondii

A plant whose leaf and seed pod are more outstanding than its flower is Drummond's dryas. It has small, yellow, drooping flowers, with a rather cowed appearance as if the heavy calyx were too much for it and the corolla could not assert itself. It is not a happy looking flower like most of the blooms of so open a situation. Its meekness vanishes, however, when the seeds begin to form. The stems elongate and the hairy tips of the seeds stretch out. Before maturity these hairs are tightly coiled and pointed upward, all in the same direction, like little sign posts that point the way. At maturity, however, they open into handsome, fluffy balls.

The leaves of Drummond's dryas are a rich, dark green above, but with a densely silvered lining. The stem is slightly dyed with red and the dark green calyx has an un-shaven look, being covered with a dark red beard.

DRUMMOND'S DRYAS and
DRYAS OCTOPETALA

These plants thrive on the poorest soil. They form mats of foliage and soft seed heads in arid mountain passes and on the windswept, gravelly rivers' edges of the lower foothills, well out onto the prairie. Their companions are great shining dragonflies that have crawled slowly from the water's edge, leaving their dry, deserted skins clinging to the rocks, while they themselves weave patterns across the ripples or race the downy seeds.

Fittingly, the plant was named by Richardson in honour of Thomas Drummond, who must have rested often by great mats of its foliage as he botanized in the lonely mountains of the Berland River country more than a century ago.

Perhaps better known, especially to the summer visitor, is the white dryas which mats the rocks of so many alpine passes. In Piegan Pass in Glacier Park and Ptarmigan Pass near Lake Louise we can see examples of its ability to hide great wastes of ugly rocks under an exquisite mantle of bloom.

The single white cup which grows close to the ground against a mat of grey-green leaves is beautiful enough to deserve the name of dryas, which is Latin for wood nymph. The only criticism possible against its name is that the flower is seldom found in the woods but likes the open sunshine. It is fond of sending its roots down into the cracks of rocks in its search for sustenance. Rock sprite might have been a name more suited to the disposition of *Dryas octopetala*.

HEDYSARUM

Another plant which is more conspicuous in seed than in bloom is the hedysarum, which is often seen on both prairie and mountain. It is unmistakably a member of the pea family, looking something like a milk vetch and growing from one to three feet high. The whole plant has a decorative appearance, the leaves being pinnate with eleven to twenty-one leaflets. The pink, creamy or purple flowers hang drooping in a long, showy spike. The seed pods are different from those of other plants of the same family, being large, scalloped and drooping also.

HEDYSARUM

EVERLASTINGS

Antennaria

A blossom that never fades has always been the dream of poets. There are many species of everlastings across the prairie and up the mountain sides and it would be hard to point a finger at one and say, "This is the most beautiful". By reason of its colour, the pink everlasting (*Antennaria rosea*) might have a slight edge, but its beauty is rivalled by the tall graceful, pearly white, slightly scented flowers of the pearly everlasting (*Anaphalis margaritacea*).

Each flower of the everlasting looks like a miniature pond lily, but the structure is quite different. Corresponding in appearance to the petals of the lily are the small white overlapping scales of the involucre, and what would be the lily's yellow stamens are, in this case, the true flowers, which become brown in drying. The leaves of all the everlastings are silvery white, the white being more marked in some species than in others. On the prairie, the everlasting grows so abundantly that it has been listed as a secondary weed.

There is an arctic everlasting, a dwarf with very white and woolly leaves and stalks that grows close to the line of perpetual snow and more nearly resembles the famous Edelweiss of the Alps than any other flower on this continent. Since the great reputation of Switzerland's national flower is chiefly due to the difficulty in obtaining it, the arctic everlasting and many of its friends of the mountain peaks may some day hold a similar place in song and story.

The popular name of cat's foot or pussy toes seems to be suggested by the furry looking tufts of the blossoms.

In the central United States a variety of *Antennaria* is called Indian tobacco and children chew the leaves. The name *Antennaria* refers to the bristles surmounting the fruit which suggest antennae.

MANY-COLOURED STARS

There is a sibilant murmur from underfoot as we walk ankle deep in freshly fallen leaves. The autumn sun streams down upon us through rows of tall white cottonwoods and high in the treetops the wind sighs through the branches, sending showers of golden leaves drifting down. Truly if the streets of heaven are paved with gold it must be the gold of newly fallen leaves from which arises the sweet tang of summer sun and frosty nights.

In such surroundings the aster is at home, reflected in some still brown pool, shining star-like against a dark recess, or twining its graceful stem through the silver tangle of fallen branches.

Aster means star, and of all the asters, the wild purple variety comes nearest to living up to its name. The pale faces on the edge of a wood seem to twinkle against the background of pine or the deep woodland shadows like stars in the summer sky. In the open woodlands, along the banks of a tiny stream, by the blue edge of a river, on the open hillside, or nodding to us from the edges of the fields, they are reminders that summer is gone and that the time of the yellow leaves is at hand.

The accurate classification of the asters is not of general interest. There are many species in our neighbourhood with very slight differences which are of interest only to the botanist. Most of them are purple or mauve but out on the dry prairies, along roadways, or in sandy soil of the cut-banks and river bottoms, the white prairie aster with its crowded panicle of bloom is as conspicuous, though lower growing, as its purple relative.

The aster, like all compositae, is made up of compact clusters of tiny

WILD ASTER

florets, the outer ones purple or pink or white, to attract the fertilizing insects. The disc or centre flowers, though comparatively few in number, add much to the character of the flowerhead. These infinitesimal flowers start life with yellow petals, but as the petal ages it turns to bright vermilion, reddish-brown or almost black. This makes a very striking combination when centres of all shades are found in the same panicle of purple-rayed flower heads.

When brought into the civilization of the flower garden, the aster forgets its delicate and graceful nature. By autumn it attains a height of fully six feet and a circumference that completely ignores the rights of its neighbours. The following spring it is usually evicted and sent to live in a corner where it can spread without trampling on the rights of others. Even so, with a tenacity of purpose worthy of a noble cause, it still appears year after year in the garden, amongst anemones, hepaticas, fritillaria and other treasures that need coaxing. In fact, it is more inclined than any other wild flower to become a weed. It spreads easily from myriads of seeds and once a root has got a start it is almost impossible to dig it out without ruining every plant in the neighbourhood. This ease of reproduction, is, of course, the culmination of aeons of evolution.

DAISY FLEABANE
Erigeron

There are also small stars which shine in the summer woods. They are the common daisies, white and purple, that in June and July scatter the western world with flowers like star dust from the milky way. These daisies may be distinguished from asters by the greater number of florets in the heads. The ray flowers are more numerous and narrower. The centre florets are so numerous that they are crowded into flat solid discs much larger in size and more compact than those of the aster. These florets are yellow and retain their colour throughout the life of the flower.

The same generations that paved the heavenly streets with gold, named these flecks of star dust fleabane, because when dried the plant was believed to have the power to drive away fleas, if powdered and sprinkled in dog kennels. The fresh herb yields an oil which is used as a remedy for skin diseases. Gathered when flowering and carefully dried, it is sold as an herb for the treatment of dropsy or for the stanching of blood.

The man who was originally responsible for the scientific name had something of the poet in his make-up. Once the flower head is fertilized by visiting insects, it quickly turns hoary-headed and so the plant was named *Erigeron* or 'early old'.

Daisy Fleabane

BLAZING STAR

Liatris scariosa

A writer on wild flowers complains that the authors of popular names do not take their responsibilities seriously enough and that many a beautiful flower is handicapped by a misleading name. Such need not be said of the *liatris* which has two very appropriate and beautiful names—blazing star and gay feather. A gay feather it is as it waves above the short grass late in August, one of the few purple flowers amongst the late summer galaxy of sun-coloured goldenrods, sunflowers and sages. And a blazing star it is when seen closely with its fringed flower heads clustering along the stem.

And now a sudden drop from poetry to the work-a-day world. As Dr. Fewster once said, some people would call an angel 'feathers'. And so some people call the blazing star 'button snake root'. Why? At the base of the plant is a small corm or root-stalk an inch or so in diameter. Some people believe the juice of this corm to be a cure for snake bite.

Examined closely, the scales surrounding the flower heads, the bracts of the involucre, are seen to be dark red in colour. As the florets open, long divisions of the style which are a vivid rose-purple are thrust out, carrying pollen to the butterflies that sip from the corolla tube.

BLAZING STAR

Strangely, it is from these style-branches rather than from the corolla that the plant takes its brilliant colour; and it is the style and not the stamens that give it the feathery appearance.

GOLDENROD

Solidago

The sunful goldenrod, John Muir called it.

> "The fragrance and the colour and the form and the whole spiritual expression of goldenrods are hopeful and strength giving beyond any others I know. A single spike is sufficient to heal unbelief and melancholy."

The goldenrods are so well known in all parts of the world that they need no description. Their scientific name refers to the curative properties attributed to them by the ancients. *Solidago* means 'making whole' or 'drawing together'. In the days of Queen Elizabeth it was in great favour for healing wounds and ulcers and was sold in powdered form. The foliage of sweet-scented goldenrod was used for making a wholesome drink.

The genus *Solidago* reaches its highest development in North America. Our largest and most handsome variety, one of the forty-three mentioned by Rydberg, is found across the continent from sea level almost to the timber-line. Poets sing with one accord of its beauty.

> Along the roadside, like the flowers of gold,
> That tawny Incas for their gardens wrought
> Heavy with sunshine droops the goldenrod.
> Whittier

In olden days it was its power to heal the wounds of the flesh that

gave it its name, but today it lives up to that name by drawing together
the wounds of the spirit.

> Graceful, tossing plume of gold,
> Waving lonely on the rocky ledge;
> Leaning seaward, lovely to behold
> Clinging to the high cliffs ragged edge.
> Burning in the pure September sky
> Spike of gold against the stainless blue
> Do you watch the vessels drifting by?
> Does the quiet day seem long to you?
>
> Matters not to you, O golden flower!
> That such eyes of worship watch you sway,
> But you make more sweet for me the dreamful hour,
> And crown for me the tranquil day.
>   Celia Thaxter

And so the moon-of-the-flowers is over. Almost before we know it the
fields are standing thick with stooks. Here and there a thresher puffs
its cloud of yellow smoke, and men, like ants against the vast horizon,
toil to gather in the harvest.

In the farm yards the great Russian sunflowers stand like old men,
their heads hung forward on their shoulders. Along the roadsides their
smaller relatives have long since faded and been mowed down. The
golden aster shares the fields with the yellow-flowered sage and along
the edge of the copses the goldenrod stands grey-headed, waiting for its
winter rest.

The mountains have burst and bubbled over with a froth of golden
leaves which has spilled out along the river bottoms to the farthest
prairies.

Out there, amongst the grey sage and ripened prairie grass, a strange
thing is happening. Down amongst the grass, at the lower tips of dead
brown leaves, are little furry bundles, curled up as yet in sleep. They
are the heads of the prairie anemone, already formed and ready for a
quick appearance in the spring. The prairie phlox, huddled close against
the ground, already holds in its mossy bosom thousands of tiny buds,

ready to open at the spring's first greeting. A little stemless daisy holds in a circlet of bracts the round buds of early spring flowers. These last two, indeed, are not so sleepy as they appear, for often in a warm November they are to be found wide awake though rather dusty.

So when the winter sends its white snow-flakes to cover up the summer, the prairie is secretly throbbing with the urgent life of the springtime, holding hands with autumn under the winter snow.

X. Berries

For us, the winds do blow,
The earth doth rest, heavens move, and fountains flow;
Nothing we see but means our good,
As our delight, or as our treasure;
The whole is either our cupboard of food,
Or cabinet of pleasure.

George Herbert

To THE WELTER of colour of the early summer flowers, the white of the berry blossoms stand as a lovely foil. The hillsides are banked with the whiteness of cherry and hawthorn, while through the river valleys stretch vistas like miniature orchards of saskatoon and tangled berry bushes.

Early summer, when the Thunderbird bringing the spring rains first rode across the prairie with flashing eyes and booming wings, was a very important season in the life of the Indian camp. In medicine tipis, sacred to Thunder and decorated with his symbols, long elaborate ceremonies were held. All the medicine men, likewise, held feasts and offered prayers to Many Drums for a good crop of berries; for, next to the meat of the buffalo, berries were the most important food of the Indians of the foothills.

SASKATOON
Amelanchier alnifolia

Because of its importance as a food and the uncertainty of its appearance, the saskatoon was the berry most in the minds of those who petitioned the Thunderbird for a plentiful crop. Some years there would be practically none, while other years the berries would hang so heavily that the slender branches would be bent to the ground and in spite of the eager depredations of men and birds, there would still be myriads left to dry on the bushes.

The berry and flower of the saskatoon both played a leading role in native ceremonies. The most important celebration of the year—the Sun Dance—was held in July, when these berries were ripe. They were used on the sacred altar and in many other ways during the week of celebration.

One of the most beautiful of simple ceremonies was the Indian custom of returning thanks to the earth for its bounty, by holding a berry aloft to the sun and then burying it in the earth. This custom of returning a gift to the earth for treasures taken from it was common to many tribes, and perhaps some of the shrubs, from which we so unthinkingly gather berries today, owe their existence to this practical form of thanksgiving.

In the tobacco-planting ceremony of the Blackfeet (a beautiful ceremony as full of mysticism as a Chinese painting) the saskatoon blossom was used to symbolize spring. The sacred vessel, which was later to carry the precious seeds to the planting ground, was filled with the blossoms of the saskatoon and the buffalo flower, more commonly known as loco weed, which turned the prairie into lakes of creamy yellow at the time the buffalo were fattest. Flowering branches of saskatoon were tied to the poles inside the chief's lodge where most of the ceremonies took place. Dry sticks were brought in to represent little human beings in the dance that was to follow. In the dance each person held a bough of saskatoon blossoms, making sweeping motions on the ground with the blooms and exclaiming at the same time to instill in the images the spirit of the earth. After dancing thus four times they stood and beat time with the branches instead of the usual rattles. Images and branches were then taken by two men and hidden near the plots where the tobacco was planted. From there the images were supposed to travel the rest of the way by themselves, turning into little boys

SASKATOON

and girls who guarded the crops during the summer months. Blossoming branches were also strewn on the way to the hiding-place.

The ripe berries formed a very important item in the menu of Indians and trappers, providing the necessary balance to a diet that would otherwise have included too large a proportion of meat. Besides eating them raw, they dried them and combined them with dried meat making a berry pemmican that was very popular. From the Indians, the white settlers soon learned their uses, canning them for winter food and drying them to replace currants which were not easily acquired in those days of oxen team freight.

David Thompson, one of the first white men to cross the prairies, gives the saskatoon a place in the journal of his travels to the Piegan country in 1787-88.

"The Misaskutum berry—perhaps peculiar to North America—
grows abundantly on willow-like shrubs. It is very sweet and
nourishing, the favourite fruit of small birds and bears. It may
safely be eaten as long as the appetite continues. The wood is
of fine size for arrows and where this can be got no other is
employed. It is weighty, pliant, non-elastic. This berry is as rich
as any currant from Smyrna and keeps as well. It ought to be
cultivated in England and Canada."

Daniel Harmon describes an interesting method of preserving
saskatoons, used by his neighbours the Carrier Indians. They made of
the bark of the spruce tree a kind of tub which would contain twenty
or thirty gallons. Into the bottom of this tub they put about a peck of
berries, and on top of them stones that were nearly red hot. They then
put in another layer of berries and another layer of stones, and so on
until the tub was nearly full. Then they covered it up and let it remain
for five or six hours until the berries were perfectly cooked. They were
then taken out and crushed between the hands, spread upon splinters
of wood tied together for the purpose and placed over a slow fire. While
they were drying, the juice which had run out while they were cooking in the tub was rubbed over them. After two or three days drying,
they were in a condition to be kept for several years. "Especially when
a few whortle berries (blue berries) are mixed with them," Harmon
says, "berries cooked in this manner are far better than those done in a
brass or copper kettle, as I have proved by repeated experiment."

Saskatoon is a name which has come to us from the Indians and trappers of the northern rivers and Manitoba. In the United States it is
called service or sarvis berry for which name there seems to be no satisfactory explanation. The French Canadian population called them
poires, because of the pear shape of some of the berries. This name,
picked up by British and American traders, became paire or pear. Unless one has previous warning, it is a bit startling to read, in the journals of a traveller in the wild north land, that the "pears are ripe and
make delicious eating".

RED-OSIER DOGWOOD

Cornus stolonifera

When Indian women picked saskatoons they always filled part of the container with a pure white berry. This berry that showed with such startling whiteness amongst the blue pomes of the saskatoons is the berry of the red-stemmed or red-osier dogwood. The Indians used it in large quantities but its bitter and acrid taste does not appeal to the white man.

In the middle of the nineteenth century Paul Kane made a trip across the mountains with the Hudson's Bay Company fur canoes, and left a very complete written and painted record. He remarks wonderingly:

> One Indian brought in some white berries which he ate eagerly but which I found very nauseous. I never saw any berry which the Indians would scruple to eat, nor have I seen any ill effects result from their doing so."

This shrub is one of the beauties of the woodland at any time of the year. In early spring the red stems, made brighter by the rising sap, cast

RED-OSIER DOGWOOD

over the woods a reddish glow that matches the robin's new spring vest. It was because of these red stems that the French Canadian population called it *bois rouge*. In June they carry fresh green leaves and many flat-topped clusters of four-parted white flowers which, like other dogwoods, are made up not of petals but of whitened bracts with invisible flowers. By July or August these have turned to clusters of snow-white or pale bluish, opaque berries which are very prominent in the dark summer woods. In autumn the leaves take on a beautiful rosy-red colour which makes a brilliant contrast to the yellows of the cottonwoods.

The bark, like that of the eastern and Pacific coast dogwoods, is bitter and tonic. The inner bark, dried in the sun or over the fire, was rubbed between the hands and broken into small pieces. In this form it was used alone or mixed with tobacco for smoking.

When held over a flame the red-stemmed dogwood oozes grease which spreads along the stem. This characteristic is explained by the story that Old Man, after roasting his meat in the coals, usually spread it to cool on the stems of the red dogwood. The stems absorbed the fat that dripped over them and they kept it there in their fibres, only to become visible when melted near a fire.

CANADIAN DOGWOOD

Cornus canadensis

Almost two hundred years ago the Canadian dogwood was being grown in English gardens as a native of Nova Scotia, although it is found in boreal haunts from Alaska and the edge of the Barren Lands to California.

Although not retiring by nature, it still holds itself aloof from the haunts of men, preferring the anxious clucking of the wood grouse and the music of small birds floating down from the tree tops. Amongst tall trees it rapidly spreads by means of underground runners, lifting myriads of clean white faces to the passerby, made all the more innocent and appealing by the frill of dark green leaves that frames them.

These very white faces are, as in all dogwoods, composed of four snowy bracts which encircle a small cluster of greenish inconspicuous flowers. These bracts fall away and each flower produces a brilliant red berry, the cluster thus formed being responsible for the familiar name of bunch berry.

These brilliant berries, together with the lovely rich autumn foliage

CANADIAN DOGWOOD

natural to the dogwoods, make the plant even more conspicuous in the autumn woods than it is in mid-summer.

The berry clusters are edible, though not appetizing to man who can usually find in their neighbourhood a much sweeter berry that is more to his taste. The birds, however, are fond of the insipid taste-lessness of it, which probably accounts for the name of pigeon berry or chicken berry by which it is often known.

KINNIKINIK

Arctostaphylos uva-ursi

When the heavily laden canoes of the fur traders crossed the threshold of the unknown west, the men took with them, as part of their pay, ten or fourteen pounds of strong tobacco done up in long rolls like the ship's perique that sailors carried with them to sea. Since all their supplies had to be carried with them, either by canoe or on their shoulders, they were fortunate to find growing in the country a plant whose leathery leaves could be added to the tobacco to make it milder and to eke out their slender supplies.

Even before the beginning of the nineteenth century, David Thompson and his fellow traders of the North West and Hudson's Bay Fur Companies had learned from the Indians to call this plant 'kinnikinik'. "The natives collect the leaves," he says. "It is mixed with

KINNIKINIK

tobacco for smoking, giving it a mild and agreeable flavour." Fifty years later Captains Lewis and Clark recorded that their *engagés* were calling it *'sacacommis'* because the *commis* or clerks of the fur companies carried it in their *sacs* or pouches.

Sir George Simpson found the Indians calling it 'atcheskapesekwa' or smoking weed and Sir James Hector recognized in this plant the smoking weed of the Scotch hills. We often read in journals of the time that the evening was spent in the making of tobacco.

The botanists ignored all this in choosing their name for the plant. This little prostrate red-berried shrub, so common on all our hillsides, boasts the generic name of *Arctostaphylos* which means bearberry. Its specific name, *uva-ursi*, also means bearberry. So there it is: family name, *Arctostaphylos;* specific name, *uva-ursi;* common name, bearberry. Three times repeated it begins to sound quite convincing.

It is not only the bears that find this flat-tasting berry irresistible. It is the favourite food of the grouse also and its fruit is borne close to the ground within easy reach of them.

The small white or pink urn-shaped flowers, growing clustered amongst the dark leathery leaves, is one of the loveliest of the springtime flowers, while in autumn the shrub produces not only bright red berries, but leaves brilliantly tinted and tipped with scarlet. The plant spreads in mats one or two yards across, from a single root.

It is often used for winter decorations. Being evergreen, it is little affected by the cold winds of winter. On the hills it may be gathered in January with the berries still fresh and red and the tips crowned with flower buds all ready to open at a moment's notice when the sun gets warm. In early spring, flowers, berries and leaves appear on a branch together.

DEVIL'S WALKING STICK

Echinopanax horridum

Dr. Cheadle and his companion Lord Milton, whom their publisher describes as the 'first transcanadian tourists', took two years in which to gratify their whim to see the Pacific Ocean by travelling overland, independently of the regular Hudson's Bay Company fur canoe traffic. In 1862-63 they crossed the continent from east to west. Leaving their Red River carts at Edmonton, they set out with horses and supplies through the Yellowhead Pass with Kamloops as their destination.

There were many difficulties encountered on the way. Their guide deserted them. The only map they possessed was the verbal direction of an old squaw. They dragged their horses through muskegs by main force only to have them roll down a precipice or be carried off by the current of a swollen river. Their luxuries, tobacco, tea, sugar and salt were soon exhausted. Their necessities became so scant that they were reduced to eating their horses—one advantage of the horse over the automobile as a means of tourist transportation. But of all these disasters the one which apparently caused the writer of the journal the greatest amount of irritation was a plant.

> Friday, July 31st—We had very harassing work, the road being so beset by red willow and the great-leaved prickly plant which trails along the ground, pierces one's moccasins and trousers and trips the horses.
> Saturday, Aug. 1st—Fallen timber up and down the mountain sides, a ground as rotten as the timber and abounding in bogs, quagmires and concealed springs. The whole so thickly covered with that infernally prickly trailer (the stems sometimes two yards long and an inch in diameter, leaves as large as a rhubarb leaf and shaped like a raspberry, bears spikes of dirty reddish green flowers, stems and leaves thickly covered with thorns like a briar) and red willows that it is impossible to see what is before you when you make your path.

What more need be said in the way of description, habitat, or the reason for the name of the plant, devil's club or devil's walking stick? To add to its malignant character the thorns are believed to be poisonous.

This same plant added one more difficulty to the many encountered by Alexander Mackenzie and his *voyageurs* in their dash to the Pacific, by way of the Peace River in 1793. The *voyageurs*, who could always be counted upon to produce a name for any plant that played a part in their daily lives and adventures called it *bois piquant*.

The decumbent stems, which led Dr. Cheadle to describe it as a trailer, turn upward at the tip, raising aloft the large palm-like leaves and a spike of brilliant red berries which make the plant a very handsome addition to the late summer woods, if viewed from the safety of a bridle path. It is a familiar plant on the eastern slopes of the mountains, though much less abundant than it is in the valleys of the western slope.

ROCKY MOUNTAIN HOLLY GRAPE
Berberis repens

Whatever the season the Rocky Mountain holly grape is easily the most conspicuous low shrub of the mountain sides, especially on dry rocky slopes or in the more open stands of pine. Its leathery leaves of deep glossy green, shaped like a glorified holly leaf, would alone

ROCKY MOUNTAIN HOLLY GRAPE

make the plant conspicuous. But in spring it is weighted with showy panicles of butter-yellow blossoms, which in their turn are almost continuously bowed beneath the weight of pollen-laden bees.

Spring, however, is not the season at which it is most attractive. By late summer the plant has produced grape-like clusters of berries covered with a bloom that is bluer than the bluest grapes. At the first approach of autumn, the polished leaves take on a gorgeous colouring that is rivalled only by the dogwoods and one or two other shrubs. The blue berries, mingling with this brilliant and shapely foliage, have been the inspiration for many designs of the Kutenai Indians as they might well be for the modern designer.

One would think that such beauty was sufficient reason for existence but the *berberis* is useful as well as beautiful. The berries make tempting jelly. The bitter bark was used by the Blackfeet as a medicine and has passed into the pharmacopoeia of modern science by reason of its tonic and laxative properties. The yellow stems have been used by the Indians of many tribes for the making of dyes.

The Oregon grape is a very similar plant, but taller growing. It is at home on the western slopes of the mountains.

WOLF WILLOW

Elaeagnus commutata

Wild roses and silver willows abloom on the banks of a stream overflowing with melted snows and yellow mud, mean that summer has come at last to the prairies.

One could not spend many weeks on the prairie at any season of the year without becoming acquainted with the wolf willow. Its densely silvery leaves are to be seen everywhere, along the streams and cutbanks, in the deep coulees of the hills, even out into the fields. In winter when the leaves are gone, its silver berries shine in the winter sun, making it more conspicuous than at any other season except, perhaps, the early summer. Then it puts forth from one to three minute, silver-coated, yellow-lined, bell-shaped flowers in the axils of the leaves. Hidden amongst the silvery leaves, they are quite inconspicuous in appearance so they draw the attention of fertilizing insects by exuding a heavy fragrance. This scent is carried for miles on the springtime breeze. So powerful is it that it needs the whole prairie in which to spread itself. Shut in, it is too overwhelming to be endured.

The colour scheme of the plant is as subtle as the perfume is strident, with its soft pale yellow and greenish-tinted silver balanced by the warm reddishness of the twigs.

When the flowers have finished their duties, the calyx tube becomes fleshy and encloses an ovary forming a berry-like fruit as silvery as the leaves. Inside the fleshy covering is a dark brown, grooved nutlet, with yellow stripes marking the channels. These nuts are quite beautiful, as the Indian women discovered. By boiling off the fleshy covering and soaking the nuts thoroughly, it is possible to pierce them and string them into a necklace. Many an Indian woman used these beads for ornaments before the glass beads of the white trader lured her to brighter colours. Holes were bored in them and a nut was run on each strand of the buckskin fringe with which she decorated her clothing. From the Indians the first white women learned their use, and many a string of these same beads has gone to old country relatives as a typical prairie gift.

In regions where it is most plentiful people still cling to the old name of wolf willow, with all its haunting memories of early days, even though they know it is not a willow but a member of the oleaster family. Wolf willow's only relative in the country is another old timer, the bull-berry.

WOLF WILLOW

BULL-BERRY

There are two kinds of buffalo-berry or bull-berry. One is *Shepherdia canadensis*, which grows in the foothills and mountains and out into moist valleys across the upper woodlands, and the other *Shepherdia argentea*, which is found in the river bottoms of the prairie regions. The first is a low, shapely bush with scaly leaves; the other has densely sil-

BULL-BERRY

very foliage, with stems broken at queer sharp angles and adorned with spines like the hawthorn.

Instead of the conventional white of the spring attire of berry society, the bull-berry has chosen a dull, brownish drab for its blossoms. These tiny flowers grow in short spikes at the joints of the leaves and appear while the leaves are just in the bud. A clump of bull-berry bushes in bloom along the moist edge of a brown pool of freshly melted snow, looks for all the world like a ruffle of time-yellowed lace from grandmother's attic.

The branches and smaller twigs stand out at angles and are terminated by villainous looking barbs. The silvery-grey branches and leaves, green on the upper surface, covered with silvery and brownish scales underneath, make the shrub inconspicuous during the summer months, but in the fall, when the fruit matures, it becomes the most beautiful and showy shrub of the western woodlands. It is because of its autumn beauty that gardeners cherish it for an ornamental shrub.

The berries are a brilliant, translucent orange-scarlet, clustering along the entire length of the branches. They have a queer, acrid, disagreeable flavour when eaten raw, but no other berry, except the saskatoon, is mentioned more often in the journals of early travellers in the west.

The Indian name for the berry signified rabbit-berry, but the fruit was used so commonly as a garnish for the buffalo steaks and roasts of the day that the *voyageurs* were soon calling it 'buffalo grease', (graisse de buffle) or 'beef fat' (graisse de boeuf). From there it was a natural step to the common names of buffalo-berry or bull-berry, when the French Canadian population began to be outnumbered by English-speaking settlers.

No old timer, even now, can live comfortably through the winter without at least a few jars of bull-berry jelly for serving with his meat. The Indians had the same idea of its usefulness for they dried the berries and used them for adding to their meat stews.

Because of the thorny spikes which protect the fruit and the determined way in which the berries cling to the stems when first ripe, the usual method of gathering them was to wait until after the first frost. Then the berries can be easily knocked from the tree onto a sheet spread beneath it on the ground.

This method, as well as the broken look of the twisted branches, are explained by a Blackfoot legend of Old Man in the days when he had ceased to be a god and had become a poor, foolish, irrational trickster.

Old Man wandered through the woods one day feeling very hungry. He came to a deep, still pool and, stooping for a drink, he beheld, lying at the bottom of the pool, a cluster of bright red berries. These were just what he wanted so he tried to reach them by diving after them. Again and again he dived into the clear water, but could not reach the bottom. Each time he stood on the bank he saw them there in the transparent depths. At last he conceived a plan which could not fail. Tearing strips of bark from the trees along the bank, he bound heavy stones about his wrists and neck and waist. Then he dived again. This time, he reached the bottom—but there were no berries there. When he decided to return to the surface, however, the stones still held him to the bottom, head down, feet floating far above. He had a desperate struggle to unloose the strings of bark but at last he threw himself half-drowned on the soft bank of the pond. As he lay there, gasping and choking for air, he looked up into the tangled branches above and there, scarcely higher than his own head, was the cluster of berries he had been diving after. Furious at having been so deceived, he seized a stick and beat the bushes until the branches were broken and the berries dropped to the ground. "Your branches will always look broken and people will always gather your berries by beating you," he told the tree. And people always have.

This story recalls another use for the shrub. The strips of bark which Old Man used to tie the stones about his wrist and waist were from the bush for whose berries he was diving. The Indians used it as a substitute, if raw hide were not available.

Having given its bark for strings and its berries for food, this strange tree turned perverse and refused its wood for firewood. 'Miss-is-a-misoi' or stink-wood, the Indians called it, and you have only to try burning it on your camp fire to understand the reason.

SNOWBERRY AND BUCKBRUSH

Symphoricarpus

Amongst the shrubbery of the river bottoms and on moist northward sloping banks, a member of the honeysuckle family makes a charming addition to the springtime blossoms and winter berries. It is best known as snowberry, though it also bears the name of wolf-berry and stag-berry. The flowers are white or pinkish bells growing in clusters at the ends of the stems and in the axils of the leaves. The berries are snow-white and so generously clustered that the branches are often bent to the ground with the weight of them. The white berry contains two dark hard seeds. It is much used as an ornamental shrub, both for the beauty of its clustered flowers in the springtime and for the weight of berries which adds beauty to the winter garden.

A somewhat similar shrub is found growing in clumps on the hill-sides of the prairies. This is the buckbrush of the prairies, though buckbrush is a term often indiscriminately applied to many low dense clumps of brush. These patches of S. *occidentalis* form shelters for many flowers of the mountains and river banks that could not otherwise endure the biting winds and drying sun of the open prairies. They are intricately branched, with greyish-brown shreddy bark on the older branches and yellowish-brown bark on the younger ones. The fruit is also white though not so plentiful as that of the snowberry.

Amongst old timers these shrubs are sometimes called water brush because they were once believed to indicate a likely spot for the drilling of the all important well, being a sign of hidden moisture just as the sage was believed to indicate soil fertility.

Snowberry

CHOKE CHERRY
Prunus melanocarpa

Choke cherries are conspicuous in the springtime for their sharp-pointed, finely-toothed, smooth green leaves and the long densely flowered racemes of sweet-scented white flowers. The fruit ripens in August, hanging in clusters of dark red, almost black berries with hard

CHOKE CHERRY

little cherry-like pits. They have an astringent quality which draws the mouth and probably accounts for the name.

Settlers soon learned to extract the juice by boiling the berries and to use it for wines and jellies. The housewife discarded the pulp and pits, and in so doing, discarded the very part that the natives treasured, for the tiny stone holds a very nutritious kernel. The Indians gathered the berries in large quantities, dried and ground them, stones and all, and added them to their pemmican, or used it to flavour soups and stews.

As a medicine it was quite as effective as the cherry tonics of grand-mother's medicine cabinet. The small twigs, stripped of their leaves and cut into pieces, were boiled in water till they produced a strong black tea of an astringent, bitter taste. It was used as a tonic and for relieving fever.

The dark purplish stems of the chokecherry are pliant and were sometimes used for bows from which were shot arrows with shafts of saskatoon wood.

FLOWERING CURRANT

Ribes aureum (Pursh)

So popular has the golden or flowering currant become as an ornamental shrub of western gardens, that it surprises most of its owners to learn that it is a native of the country. Its name was given it by that same Frederick Pursh who first named our gaillardia. As it is mentioned continually in the Lewis and Clark journals, it is reasonable to believe that it was one of the specimens collected by Captain Lewis and turned over to Pursh for study and naming. It was originally known amongst the traders and *engagés* as Indian currant or Buffalo currant.

In early spring the shrub, growing from four to eight feet high,

WILD CURRANT

bursts into a perfect glory of small golden blossoms each of which, to add to its perfection, has a perfect crimson eye. These flowers are replaced by large, sweet-tasting berries, usually of clear amber yellow, though sometimes of black or red.

In August the shrub breaks into strange new blossom, being literally bowed down beneath the weight of open-mouthed, speckle-breasted robin nestlings and anxious parents who stuff their offspring with sweet currants. Later in the year, when the snow is on the ground, and withered berries still cling to the shrub though all the leaves have gone, it becomes host to a squealing, ravenous horde of waxwings and by spring is ready, once more, to burst into yellow bloom.

It is a matter of individual taste whether the berries are used for jelly for the household or are left to produce their succeeding crops of autumn and winter birds. The currants make a very delicately flavoured jelly and have been used by thrifty housewives, both Indian and white.

HONEYSUCKLE

Honeysuckles, well known in all parts of the country and to all ages, are interesting to us chiefly because of certain unusual habits of growth.

The smooth-leafed honeysuckle is the woodbine of Milton and Scott. Shakespeare's "bank where the wild thyme grows" was "quite over-canopied with lush woodbine", and must have been a background suitable to such a fantasy as *A Midsummer Night's Dream;* for the woodbine is a trailing shrub that gently enfolds the rocks and tree trunks around which it grows. "I will wind thee in my arms. So doth the woodbine, the sweet honeysuckle entwist", says Queen Titania to Bottom the weaver.

Smooth leaves covered with a delicate bloom grow along its twining stem in pairs. The top pair of leaves joins to encircle the stem forming a deep green bowl to hold the trumpet-shaped flowers which are an attractive blending of coral and yellow. Later the green bowl holds a group of bright red berries which, though not pleasing to the human palate, are loved by the birds.

Closely related to this woodbine is the bush or fly honeysuckle,

HONEYSUCKLE

sometimes known as twinberry. (Twins apparently run in families because, remember, the twin flower is a honeysuckle also.) The twinberry does not trail but grows upright as a compact, bushy shrub. The twin yellow flowers are conspicuously involucred by large, leaf-like bracts. It is the berries, however, that attract attention. They are black and shiny, joined together like Siamese twins and still surrounded by the showy bracts which have turned bright red or purplish.

RASPBERRY

Rubus strigosa is the variety of raspberry most common across the entire northern part of the continent. As many of the excellent market varieties owe their origin to this hardy native no one can mistake it for other than what it is. It has been a mainstay in the fruit line to Indians and pioneers alike, newcomers recognizing and eagerly welcoming it as a reminder of home.

Much more showy in our woods is *Rubus parviflorus*, flowering raspberry, thimbleberry or salmonberry. (Julia Henshaw calls it cap berry). It is a handsome plant that spreads its coarse foliage to form a waist-high undergrowth through open woodlands, and tops it with beautiful flowers of crinkled white tissue. The leaves are broad and coarsely veined, the flowers like miniature white roses. When the petals drop, a fruit forms that looks like a luscious, pale red raspberry but tastes flat and woody, belying the promise of the flowers.

Another showy member of the family is the *Rubus spectabilis*, sometimes also called salmonberry. The flowers are reddish-purple or rose-coloured. The fruit lives up to the promise of the flowers. It is yellow or red with a sweet juice that made it a favourite with the original inhabitants. Another pink-flowered member of the tribe is the arctic raspberry which grows to an altitude of 8,000 feet and follows the cold climate far into the arctic regions.

In sphagnum bogs grows a quaint little raspberry whose fruit is sometimes mentioned in early reports of the northern part of the country. A single dainty white flower is pushed a short way above the moss on a stem adorned with two large, coarse leaves of typical raspberry pattern. A berry forms on the pistillate bloom which reverses the usual order by turning from green to red and then to yellow when ripe. Its peculiar, pleasant flavour is responsible for the name of baked-apple berry.

ELDER-BERRY

Sambucus

The elder-berry is a perfect example of a plant native to this country, yet similar enough to the European species to have inherited all the heaped-up legend and superstition of the old world. For some reason or another, the elder seems to have come in for more than its share.

For instance, if you have ever wished for the strength of thirty men, the elder-berry and the devil may be able to help you. On the night of January 6th you should stand before an elder shrub and ask permission to cut a branch. If no answer comes from the wood you must spit three times, then cut a branch. With it mark a magic circle in a lonely field, stand at the centre and demand of the devil that he give you some of his precious fern seed that will give you the strength of thirty men. On that particular night, and if all instructions are carefully carried out, the devil must obey if only you point at him the wand of elder's wood.

This alone should ensure the elder a high place in our regard, but it can do many other things besides. Here and there in my reading I have found the following uses. Elderwood cures toothache and freckles and colds, keeps the house from attack, fends off snakes, mosquitoes and warts; it quiets nerves, interrupts fits, keeps worms out of furniture, curls hair, guarantees a long life and assures that he who cultivates it shall die in his own home. An eighteenth century gardener recommends that cabbage and cauliflower be whipped with elder twigs to preserve them from insects, and an infusion of elder leaves is still used today to keep bugs from vines.

In the Tyrol, where peasants lift their hats to the elder, they plant an elder cross on a grave. When it bursts into bloom and leaf it is a sign that the departed one has found happiness beyond. Skinner, who reported this in his book on myths and legends, adds slyly, "If, however, it fails to grow, relatives may draw their own conclusions."

The scientific name for the elder, *Sambucus,* is said to have been derived from the sambuke, an ancient musical reed instrument. The stem of the elder has a soft inner pith which is easily removed, leaving a hard yellow stem. The Indians and *voyageurs* of the north removed the pith and dried the stems for pipe stems.

Sanders, in his book on California wild flowers, says that among the California Indians the tree is known as 'the tree of music'. He relates how the grandson of Coyote Man heard the music the trees made, and begged the old women who guarded them for a twig, from which he planted trees all through the western world.

Like the strawberry and raspberry, the native elders are so similar to the familiar species that they are easily recognised. They are low shrubs, growing up to eight or ten feet high. The compound leaves are divided into from five to seven leaflets and the graceful stems are topped with fragrant, creamy flowers growing in a rounded cluster. The fruit is tart and edible. Though it may be eaten raw it is usually made into pies or wines.

MOUNTAIN ASH

In the old country the mountain ash or rowan tree belongs near buildings, especially about barns and cattle sheds, since to it was attributed the power to protect animals from witchcraft. In fact one of its popular names is witch wood.

Here, however, it is a decorative thing, its orange-red berries making

MOUNTAIN ASH

brilliant splashes of colour against the solemn blues and blacks of the evergreens on rocky hillsides and in ravines. In spring it tosses huge cymes of creamy white flowers in the breeze. In autumn it is a thing to dream about with the great compound leaves turned yellow and copper in rivalry to the scarlet berries. But perhaps in winter after the leaves have dropped it reaches its greatest beauty, the snow and black masses of evergreens weaving such a colourful pattern with its scarlet fruit.

The mountain ash is not really an ash at all but belongs to the apple family, though it does not share with the other members of the family their delightful appeal to the human palate. It is a variety of the well known rowan tree of Scotland where they make a jelly of its berries. Here, however, perhaps because of the wealth of tastier berries, it is little used. In fact the reproachful name of dogberry is sometimes applied.

But if it does not tickle the human palate, at least the flavour is not distasteful to the birds. In the winter roving bands of Bohemian waxwings, with their blue-grey bodies and bands of red and yellow on wing and tail, visit the trees. Squealing and chattering, they can strip a heavily laden tree in only a few days, working at it from early morning until the last ray of twilight. Early returning robins pick up the few remaining berries that were dropped in the snow.

WILD STRAWBERRY

"Doubtless God could have made a better berry, but doubtless He never did," was Izaak Walton's well known verdict on the strawberry; and who should know better the flavour of wild strawberries than that philosophic fisherman.

While the cultivated variety has been increased in size, no addition has been made to the flavour. Most of us would agree with Macaulay who exclaimed, on his return from India, that he would gladly trade all the fruits of the Orient for a single basket of strawberries.

Old Man has planted his garden very generously with these luscious berries. Many varieties are found through the mountains and across the prairies, all looking so much like strawberries that no one but a botanist even thinks of variety.

The berry, of course, is not a berry in the technical sense, for it lacks the outer skin enclosing seeds and pulp that distinguishes the true berry. It is a fleshy, swollen, seed receptacle bearing dry, yellow seeds upon its pitted outer surface. The star-shaped hull that is removed before the berry is eaten was, at flowering time, the calyx.

BLUEBERRY AND CRANBERRY

"The common huckleberry, oftener seen in pies and muffins by the average observer than in its native thickets, unfortunately ripens at fly time, when the squeamish boarder in the summer hotel does well to carefully scrutinize each mouthful." So Neltje Blanchan begins the huckleberry, blueberry and cranberry section in her book on eastern wild flowers.

Such are the joys and trials of civilization. To James Hector, who broke five days of enforced fasting in the Kicking Horse Pass when he came across a patch of blueberries, to Daniel Harmon, David Thompson, Alexander Mackenzie and many others who staved off starvation with them, they were connected with neither flies nor pies, but were in themselves deliciously nourishing meals.

Huckleberry, whortleberry, bilberry, blueberry are names applied to members of the huckleberry family that are so closely related as to be almost indistinguishable. Usually the blacker berries are referred to as huckleberries while the bluish one with the pale bloom are called blueberries. By whatever name we know them, and whatever the specific name, we know that in pies or muffins, or raw with a garnish of cream, they are hard to beat.

There are two berries popularly known as cranberries. The true cranberry is a denizen of swamps and marshy places. It is a delicate little trailing vine with small leaves that are dark green above and white beneath. The four or five tiny, narrow pink divisions of the corolla are pendant from slender, swaying stems and are as pretty as the round red fruit.

Cranberries are members of the huckleberry family and justly popular in the kitchen. Frederick V. Coville, however, draws a fine distinction between them and their near relatives. The blueberry, he says, has the cranberry beaten "because you can't use cranberries without buying a turkey." This distinction would not trouble a pioneer who would just go out and shoot whatever wild game he fancied.

The other type is known as the high bush, mountain or Swedish cranberry and is especially plentiful through the northern sections. This berry grows on low shrubs. Its leaves are thick, dark green and shiny above, pale and black dotted beneath, with curled margins. Growing as it does in rocky places and open woods, and about two feet off the ground, it is more easily gathered and in more common use as a wild fruit than the true cranberry.

WILD GRAPE

The wild grape creeps into our territory from the eastern region. It was mentioned in old journals when the travellers paused a moment at Fort Garry before entering the wilderness, or as they pushed slowly up the Missouri into the dangerous Blackfoot country, and then never again until they reached that point on their homeward journey.

Two stories told by Lewis and Clark are interesting. The first refers to the origin of the Mandan tribe.

The whole tribe once resided in one large underground village near a subterranean lake. They knew nothing but the darkness until a grape vine extended its roots down to their habitation and gave them a view of the light. Some of the most adventurous climbed up the vine and were delighted with the sight of the earth, which they found covered with buffalo and rich with every kind of fruit. They returned with the grapes they had gathered, and their countrymen were so pleased with the taste of them that the whole nation resolved to trade their dull existence for the charms of the upper region. Men, women and children ascended by means of the vine; but when about half the tribe had reached the surface of the earth a corpulent woman who was clambering up the vine broke it with her weight, and closed herself and the rest of the nation from the light of the sun. When Mandans die they hope to return to the land of their forefathers, but only the good reach the village by means of the lake. The burden of the sins of the wicked will not permit them to cross it.

A few miles back from the Missouri River, Captain Lewis discovered two stones resembling human figures and a third a dog. The story told of them would, as he says, "adorn the *Metamorphoses* of Ovid". A young man was deeply enamoured of a girl whose parents refused their consent. Accompanied by his faithful dog, the youth went out into the fields to mourn his misfortune, and sympathy of feeling led the lady to the spot. After wandering together and having nothing to subsist on but grapes, they were at last converted into stone, and nothing was left unchanged but a bunch of grapes which the lady holds in her hands to this day. Whenever the Indians pass these stones they stop to make some offering of dress to propitiate these deities. There is an abundance of grapes in the neighbourhood.

MORE BERRIES

Besides those already mentioned there were many other berries that played a part in the daily life of the people who were entirely dependent on the products of the country.

There was, for instance, the gooseberry and the currant; the haw-thorn whose lovely blossoms cover the steep slopes of the river banks with English 'may' in June. The berries of this shrub are edible though not very tasty. The branches furnished the hardest wood in the coun-try and were used by the Crees for the pegs in their wooden carts.

These berries formed as important a crop for the Indian as wheat does for the white man. It seems little to be wondered at that in the spring, at the time of the first thunder, the medicine men and all the people prayed—"Listen Sun! Listen Thunder! Listen Old Man! All Above Animals and Above People, listen! Pity us! Let us not starve. Give us rain during the summer. Make the berries large and sweet. Cover the bushes with them. Look down on us all and pity us. Let us live."

It was a prayer with as much dignity and urgency as the Christian— "Send us we beseech thee, in this our necessity, such moderate rains and showers, that we may receive the fruits of the earth to our comfort."

XI. Trees

For he's bewitched forever who has seen,
Not with his eyes but with his vision, Spring
Flow down the woods and stipple leaves with sun.
                                        V. Sackville-West

A Great Medicine

ONCE THE trees and Indians could talk together in a language both could understand. But that was long ago. The great old chiefs of the Indians died but the trees continued to live. They made friends with the new chiefs who grew old and died but still the trees lived on; and after a while they learned to withdraw themselves from the transient company of men, holding whispered conversations together far up near the calm blue skies, while down among their roots the pygmy race of men went on with its living and dying. The Indians no longer understood what the trees whispered—nor cared, being occupied with their little affairs. The solemn trees gave scarcely more thought to the race of men than to the squirrels that hid nuts in their branches.

Only in dreams did the trees talk to men.

Only occasionally did some man come to listen to their stories with that inward ear that could understand the aged mutterings of the centuries-old pines or the garrulous chatter of the youthful poplars.

In those long-ago days when men and trees were still friends and the gods walked the earth amongst them, a great trial was laid upon the trees. They were required by the Great Chief of the forest to attend

a council where they were to remain awake for seven days and seven nights.

Some of the trees remained awake faithfully to the end, but for others the task was too strenuous and they failed. These weaker ones were punished by the Great Chief by being compelled to lose their hair (what greater punishment could an Indian chief devise?) and to shiver in the icy blasts of winter without their clothes.

The promise was made, however, that each spring, when the flowers bloomed, their hair should be given back to them. The successful contestants were allowed not only to keep their hair but were provided, every winter, with a mantle of white fur to protect them from the cold wind.

QUAKING ASPEN

Aspen tremuloides

The aspen never really recovered from the terrible ordeal of the council. Even today, when the fir tree stands in the drowsy peace of a summer siesta, the highly strung aspen is all aquiver, set astir by some imperceptible tiny breeze. This tremulous attitude towards life has been taken into account in its scientific name of *Aspen tremuloides*.

Its delicate, green-lit gown and yielding figure weaves in and out amongst the formal black of the manly pines on all the lower mountain slopes. It lives in groves on the valley floor, wherever it can find sufficient moisture. Crowds are decidedly not to its liking and so it is found growing in sunlit open groves where flowers bloom and the graceful deer come feeding amongst the dewdrops of the early dawn.

In spring, the trees burst first into a hazy froth of short greyish catkins loved of the early bees. The trees are of two kinds, staminate and pistillate, and are fertilized by these busy seekers after wax. Then the tiny seeds are wrapped in a covering of white cotton and a summer snow storm of soft white down falls over the bursting buds of the summer still to come. The trees, however, do not depend entirely on their seeds for reproduction, but also on the sprouts sent up by the parent tree.

The trunk is covered with soft greenish white bark. As the tree grows upward, the lower branches die and break off leaving a little black eye and eye-brow wherever a branch has been. Old scratches and cuts are also covered with a black scar so that the older trees have a mottled, pocked appearance.

When Old Man taught his people the use of the plants of the prairie and the trees of the mountains, he did not forget to mention the aspen. The soft inner bark was eaten raw or roasted, and probably saved many an Indian life during the famine year when the buffalo first disappeared from the plains.

The aspen is a healer like the fireweed, being the first tree to find its way to newly burnt ground or slashing. Compared with other trees the aspen poplar is very short lived having an average span of only about fifty years.

BALM OF GILEAD

No scent is so typical of spring as the resinous, spicy fragrance of the big brown buds of the balm of Gilead. It is not surprising that the Indians, who had no craving for the sickly sweetness of European perfumes, gathered these buds into little buskskin bags for scent.

The name balm of Gilead, which was given because of this resinous tang, was really borrowed from the Bible. The balm mentioned there is the gum or resin from the trunk of a tree found in the mountainous district of Gilead in southern Syria and referred to by Bible historians as the Balm out of Gilead.

Our balm of Gilead, or western balsam poplar, is a handsome tree with erect, stout branches and grey trunk, which grows to a height of one hundred feet. The twigs are thick jointed and gnarled, showing the scar of every fallen leaf.

In the spring the buds are covered with a fat golden brown sheath that falls away as the catkin opens out. When the catkin first bursts from its clasping bud, it is a dark, amazingly rich maroon, but it becomes bright red and then pale green with reddish tips as it lengthens out. When at last the flowers have had their day, they fall with a thud like a heavy green worm that has let go its hold in the treetops.

When the first birds come north in the spring, they are ravenous hordes come from a land of plenty to a land of starvation. Everything they see is potential food. To such hungry wayfarers the early catkins

BALM OF GILEAD

of the poplars and willows are like manna in the desert and the trees play host to hundreds of these hungry transients.

The tree was called by the Indians 'the ugly poplar' in allusion to its tough bark and naked stem, crowned in an aged state with a few distorted branches.

Franklin reports that a decoction of the resinous buds was sometimes successfully used by the Indians in cases of snow-blindness but its application to the inflamed eye caused much pain.

COTTONWOOD

A companion of the balm of Gilead in the river bottoms of the west is the cottonwood, also a member of the poplar family. The young trees have smooth, pale bark but that of the older trees is dark and deeply ridged. It is a rapid grower, attaining a height of seventy-five or a hundred feet and a diameter of several feet. At one time, it is believed, there were extensive forests of this poplar where now there is only prairie, but fire and drought took toll of them until now they are found only in the river bottoms.

The ancient trees of the mountain-sides were ageless and aloof, but in these rapid growing poplars the Indians felt a personal interest. The old, deeply grooved, shady cottonwoods were the friends of the old people, while the children were taught not to harm the young white saplings so that they, the trees and the children, might grow up together to be friends in their old age.

When the first white settlers camped in the river valleys of the west, many an old cottonwood held in its arms the last resting place of a famous chief or the weary bones of a medicine woman, but the lives of the poplars are short. These markers of forgotten burial places have fallen and been carried off on springtime floods and a new generation of trees has grown up to shelter the strange ideals of a new race of men.

WILLOWS

Along the river banks and up the mountain slopes grow willows of all sizes. They range from trees of sixty or eighty feet to the tiny willows, which are classified as shrubs, but grow above the timber-line to a height of only three or four inches. These bear catkins of the same generous size as the sixty foot trees.

Many species of willow form the summer tangle of green along the

WILLOWS

banks of streams, but are scarcely noticed except as a background for cool waters or bright flowers. Only in spring does the willow really come into its own, when soft grey catkins are found long before the first spring flowers; or showy yellow ones form a golden aureola round a dark brown pool and add a brighter note to the green tapestry of the springtime hills.

The seed pods which follow these earliest of flowers each bear a tuft of silky white hair, and the white 'willow cotton' which drifts hither and thither on the late spring breeze is a more conspicuous part of the springtime landscape than the willows themselves. Indian mothers gathered this silken down to line the cradles of their babies, padding them as softly as the inside of a humming bird's nest. The young shoots or osiers were also used for making baskets and comfortable backrests for use in tipis or for the 'cradles' stretched across the poles of the travois.

Along northern rivers and lakes, where the Indians depended on fish for food, they used the inner bark of the willow for making nets. They always kept on hand a large quantity of the fibre, which they worked into thread on their thighs. These nets measured from eighteen to two hundred feet in length and from thirteen to thirty-six inches in depth.

The bark contains a large percentage of tannin and so was a valuable tanning material. A medicine, known today as salicin, is also extracted from the bark of willows and is used in the treatment of rheumatic fever and neuralgia. Alexander Mackenzie records that practically the only medicine known to the northern tribes was the bark of the willow which, being burned and reduced to a powder, was applied to green wounds and ulcers.

LODGE POLE PINE

Almost every year the poles which supported the buffalo skin lodges of the prairie Indians had to be replaced. Moving about from place to place, following the buffalo or the ripening berries, the Indians used the lodge poles as vehicles of transport, the thinner ends being placed over the necks of the horses, the thicker ends being laced across with willow-work lattices that carried the household bundles. Dragging over the prairie quickly wore the ends of the poles until they were too short, either for travois poles or lodge poles.

Fortunately Old Man placed great forests of pines within easy reach of most of the tribes. These pines follow quickly on the heels of the fireweed and the aspen in their work of covering burnt areas, their tall, slender trunks forming dense groves on the easily accessible lower slopes of hills and mountains, and swaying alarmingly in every slight breeze. The regular use of these tall trees by the Indians has suggested the common name of lodge pole pine.

The pine may be recognized by the short leaves, in bundles of two, the small spreading cones, which often remain on the tree for several years, and the scaly, greyish-brown bark which is lighter orange on

LODGE POLE PINE

the branches. Altogether it is one of the commonest trees of the Rockies, being especially abundant at lower altitudes on the eastern slopes, and reaching from Alaska in the north, southward to California and east to Manitoba.

WHITE PINE

One of the most common of the trees up near the timber-line is the white bark pine. Rarely growing more than twenty-five feet, like the balsam fir which shares the upper mountains with it, it often becomes a dwarfish, stunted shrub. The creamy scales of the bark make the trunks white, somewhat resembling the balsam. It has dark, purplish-brown cones, which grow horizontally, close against the stalk.

The seeds of most evergreens are loved by the birds; but this pine has especially large and succulent seeds which the Indians used for food.

The Indians made strong, fine thread from the fibrous roots of the white pine. This thread, Alexander Mackenzie tells us, was called 'watape' and was used for sewing together the sheets of birch bark used in the making of canoes. A quantity of this watape was always included amongst the supplies carried on a long canoe journey. The Indians also made vessels of it in which they cooked their food. These were in the shape of a gourd, narrow at the top and wide at the bottom and were woven in such a manner as to hold water, which was made to boil by putting into it a succession of red hot stones. The vessels varied in size from those with a capacity of one to two gallons for ordinary use to those capable of holding as much as sixty gallons for ceremonies.

The flavour of food cooked in vessels made from roots and bark did not always appeal to the white man. "The fish", one writer remarks, "would have been excellent if it had not tasted of the kettle, which was made of the bark of white spruce, and of the dried grass with which it was boiled." Daniel Harmon, however, thought that they improved the flavour of saskatoons.

THE LONE PINE

Old Man and Old Woman

As Old Man wandered over the prairie one day he came upon . . . a camp of women. He stood on the bank and laughed and laughed, for he had made these women himself—and then forgotten about them!

He had made them and taught them all they knew. He had taught them how to make a piskun of rocks and to lure the buffalo into it, to drive them over the bank, and to kill, with a large rock, any that still survived. He had taught them how to skin the buffalo with a sharp stone and to tan the hide—but wait a minute!

They seemed to have learned a little for themselves. They were all dressed in tailored dresses made of fine soft skins neatly sewn and decorated. Old Man thought of the men up there in the camp on the banks of the Bow. He had made them too and taught them how to make bows and arrows. They could run far out over the prairie and bring back buffalo hides and meat. But they were dressed in hard, rough old buffalo hides and lived in uncomfortable lodges.

Old Man sniffed. Something smelled good. The women had learned to cook. Old Man threw back his head and laughed again. His women had learned a thing or two but he had an idea!

He clambered down the banks and asked for the chief of the women. Old Woman came to him. She was one of those straight backed, stolid women. She was not afraid of Old Man, nor of any one else for that matter. Old Man admired her tremendously and felt quite humble in her presence.

He suggested that, since the men were such very good hunters and the women such very good home-makers, they should get togther. If each woman had a hunter and each man had a lodge-keeper every one should be very happy.

Old Woman rather liked the idea, especially as buffalo were sometimes hard to get, so she told Old Man to bring his men to the river bank that the women might go up, one at a time, and choose themselves mates.

Old Man went to the valley of the Bow and bringing the men with him, he lined them up on the banks of the Old Man River. In the meantime Old Woman had been doing some thinking. She had been fooled by Old Man before. Remember the time he had let her throw the stone into the river? He had said, "If it floats we shall all live forever and there will be no death." As if a stone would ever float! But she had been very new to the world then and didn't know. She would not be fooled again.

She suspected that what Old Man wanted was some one to do the work for him, to be cook and housekeeper; but she was equally certain that he would do no hunting for her if he could get out of it. So she dressed herself in an old ragged buffalo hide, one of those she had made long ago when she first learned to sew, and she went up first to choose a mate.

She walked straight up to Old Man and said she would have him.

Old Man squirmed. He had set his heart on having the head woman, the cleverest of the lot, and he was not going to be passed off on any ragged old beggar.

Old Woman returned to the river bottom and donned her elk-skin dress with all the trimmings. Then she went again to the river bank and walked up and down the line of men. Old Man was very excited. He dodged about, falling over his own feet and getting under hers, making himself as conspicuous as possible. But Old Woman apparently did not see him for she chose herself another mate.

Then all the women came and chose themselves mates. But obeying Old Woman's instructions, they all passed by Old Man, till finally all the men and all the women had mates—except Old Man.

Then Old Woman felt sorry for lonely Old Man, so she turned him into a pine tree, telling him that he would always have food without working for it, a well tailored suit and a large feather head-dress.

Old Man was sad at first, but when he saw the women driving the men to hunt and fight, when they would much rather lie around sleeping and smoking, he began to laugh again.

All down through the ages he has laughed as he sat there on the bank of the Old Man River with the wind whistling through his hair. When men were not quarrelling with their wives they were fighting the Snakes and Kutenais. When the Snakes and Kutenais were vanquished, the white man came. The Indians were put in reserves, there under his very eyes. They were not allowed to fight any more and had nothing to do but to quarrel with their wives.

It was the white men now who showed feverish activity. They rode in bright red coats past Old Man. They tore up the land and laid long glistening rails, and on the rails, with incredible speed, travelled a new kind of horse. Men rode on this horse past Old Man and did not see him, they were in such a hurry.

Then they hauled great loads of gravel. They dumped it in long straight lines right under his very toes. They ploughed and scraped and measured and rolled and made such a tremendous fuss and bustle! And when they were finished, sleek pompous men rolled by in sleek pompous cars over a new hard-surfaced motor road.

Old Man thought of the travois that, long ago, had travelled this same road on just such important business, and he threw back his head and laughed again as the wind roared through his hair. For faster than the wind flew these sleek new cars on this straight new road, saving time for these sleek pompous men.

And what do you think these men were doing with the time they were saving? What was there for them to do in this desolate country, on the edge of the Rockies, where there was nothing to see but wind swept trees? What was there for them to do but to quarrel with their wives?

BALSAM FIR

The Balsam fir is a shrub of the timber-line, that magic place where summer and winter meet and live side by side for several months of the year. Mingled with the exquisite clearness of the sunshine and brittle air is the fragrance of the balsam.

Below the timber-line the balsam fir is a fine tall tree but it gradually diminishes in size as it climbs, until it becomes a stunted shrub. But in the driest, most rugged spots, its fragrance increases and it holds upright, within easy reach, a crowded crown of blue-purple-black cones which one cannot miss seeing. They are unlike the cones of any other evergreen and are an instant clue to the tree's identity. They are quite 'rubbery', looking like bits of old tires.

The bark on older trees is scaly, but on younger ones it is smooth and warty, being covered with blisters filled with resin. Woodsmen, far from corner drug stores, lift out these capsules from the bark and carry them about, unbroken, until they are needed for the closing of a cut or wound.

Perhaps it was from the Indians that the white men first learned its uses. They used it for colds on the chest and for a poultice to reduce fever. By mixing it with grease, they obtained a delightful aromatic hair oil.

Commercially this resin is used in perfumes, confections and med-

CANADA BALSAM

icines, chiefly in the manufacture of lozenges for throat troubles. This same balsam family supplies the well known turpentine, 'Canada balsam', and is used for making a varnish which, because of its transparency, is a valuable cement for optical instruments and spectacles.

In every ceremony except the Sun Dance, its fragrant needles were used at times to replace sweet grass as an incense. For this purpose the leaves were dried and stored.

> "Before starting the ceremony for curing the sick, the old medicine woman, removing a coal from the fire, placed dried sweet balsam upon it and holding her hands in the smoke, prayed to the spirit of the buffalo, that she might be able to discover where the disease lay."

JUNIPER

The junipers are included by botanists amongst the trees and shrubs. Though the tallest is a tree, from ten to fifty feet in height, the lowest of the species boasts a height of only a few inches.

All junipers carry a globose cone resembling a berry. These berries are bright blue, covered with a whitish bloom and are quite sweet. They are a favourite food of the birds, while old timers used them in the making of a sweet wine.

The branches of the juniper were used in the Sun Dance ceremony of the Blackfeet, the altar of the sacred woman being made in the soft earth and lined with juniper.

Two species were quite common in Old Man's territory and are often mentioned in early journals. One, *Juniper sibirica*, is a typical juniper with leaves standing out from the stem in whorls. The other seems to be a cross between a juniper and a cedar, having the flat, scale-like leaves of the cedar and the blue berries of the juniper. In some botanies it is listed as *Juniper horizontalis,* and in others as a cedar, *Sabina horizontalis.*

Both these shrubs are used in modern gardens for ground covers.

PAPER BIRCH

This tree is found scattered here and there over the whole of the prairie and foothill regions, but is especially abundant on the rivers and lakes of the north. It is the tree from which the Indians of northern and eastern Canada made their canoes and birch-bark vessels. Trees large enough for making canoes are found almost to the northernmost limits of Alberta and Saskatchewan. From there they gradually diminish in size to the edge of the Barren Lands.

Birch, being the only hardwood of the region, was used in the manufacture of snow shoes, sleighs and so on, as well as for axles of the wooden wheeled carts. The tough roots were fashioned by the clever fingers of the early settlers into pipes, which were easily lost on the trail but difficult to replace when the nearest commercial source of supply was many hundreds of miles away.

A fungus, found growing on the birch trees of the west, was gathered and dried in large quantities by the Indians, who used it for keeping alive the fire which they carried from camp to camp, or as tinder to light new fires when away from home. This fungus was known as 'touchwood' and was very abundant in the Touchwood Hills.

Another quite obvious use for the tree was the use of the inner barks for notes and letters, when the precious supply of paper was lost or damaged. Many stories are told to explain the thin, peeling bark of the tree and its ragged, torn appearance, so different from other trees, but for sheer originality none can compare with the story told by the prairie Indian.

Old Man had a favourite game that he played with the animals of the woods and prairies. He would lie down by the fire and let the animals cover him up with warm ashes. When he became too hot he would cry out and the animals would uncover him. Then he, in turn, would bury them, and when they yelled that they were too hot, he would heap more ashes on them and leave them there to roast, and so would have a pleasant feast.

One day when he was playing this game with the squirrels, the fire burned him. He was so uncomfortable that he called upon the wind to blow. The cool breeze made him feel better, so he continued to call until the gale attained such force that he was blown away.

As he flew through the air, he caught hold of a pine tree, but it was pulled out by the roots. He caught the branch of an aspen and a willow and a poplar, but out they all came by the roots, and on he flew over the prairie.

At last he seized the top of a birch tree. Its stem was so strong and its roots were so tough that it could not be broken or uprooted and Old Man was pulled, at last, to the ground.

When he got back his breath and was rested, Old Man became angry with the birch for having such strong roots that it could not be pulled up like other trees. He was having a good time being blown about by the wind, he said, and the birch tree had spoiled his fun. So angry was he, in fact, that he drew his stone knife from his belt and gashed the birch all over.

MEDICINE TREES

Indians have always regarded trees as possessing a medicine more powerful than the other plants of the earth. Before the coming of the white man, the prairies were often set afire for a very slight reason—a signal to a friend, to drive the game in a certain direction, to clear the prairie of hay and make it green and tempting to the buffalo. Many groves of fine young saplings and even woods of full grown trees were destroyed in this manner. But occasionally some lone tree would be possessed of so strong a medicine that it would escape, year after year, from the fire magic, until it became so venerable and so powerful that it was known throughout the entire country and received gifts and prayers from every passing band. One large willow had its top bound into a bunch. Many offerings of value were made to it. It was mentioned as an instance of its power that a sacrilegious deer, having ventured to crop a few of its tender branches, was found dead at a distance of a few yards.

There is a tree which has affected more lives than any other tree, but it is not mentioned in the average botany. It is known as the Tree of the Knowledge of Good and Evil. We are accustomed to thinking of this tree as belonging only to one part of the globe, the garden of Eden. Yet a similar tree is said to have grown on a beautiful island in a northern lake. On this tree Good and Evil hung suspended.

Two brothers lived with their father on this happy island. Their father told them, "Here is a great abundance of game and fruit. Hunt and eat as much as you like but do not, under any circumstances, eat the unripe fruit." But to the younger brother, the unripe fruit looked more tempting than anything else on the island, so he reached out his hand and plucked the unripe fruit and ate it.

The Old Man was very angry and sent the two boys out into the world, where they and their children have lived unhappily ever since.

Moon-When-the-Leaves-Turn-Yellow

The fluttering of yellow leaves to their sodden winter beds is a subject loved by poets of all ages, but to the Indian goes the credit for the loveliest of all autumn stories. So exquisite is its imagery, so universal its setting, that it has been accredited to many tribes.

Cold Maker, who lives far beyond the country of the Crees, in the land where the Spirits (Northern Lights) dance, was very angry with the People of the Plains. Swooping down on them as they slept in their buffalo skin lodges, he pelted them with white snow arrows and bitter winds, until they went to the trees for refuge. The trees spread out their bright gold leaves and hid the people.

Howling and shrieking with rage, Cold Maker tore the leaves from the trees and hurled them, one by one, to the ground. The people were sad when they saw the trouble they had brought to the trees, and they wept, begging Old Man to put the leaves back on the branches again. But Old Man shook his head. "Cold Maker's medicine is powerful", he said. "I cannot put the leaves back on the trees. But I will give them wings and then they can fly to a land where Cold Maker cannot follow."

Then he gave wings to the leaves of the willows and cottonwoods and they flew about amongst the trees. They became yellow birds, the warblers, the finches and the orioles. To the rose leaves and dogwoods he gave wings and the woods were filled with robins and grosbeaks, with bay-breasted warblers and purple finches. Such a fluttering they made as they slipped through the woods, dressing the bare boughs again in the brightest colours!

There was one little leaf—a grey colourless little thing, who was so excited that he flew straight up to the blue covering of the Sun Chief's Lodge and came away with some of the dye on his wings.

When the lonely keening of little birds floats down through the blackness of an autumn night, it is really the eerie song of lost leaves winging southward on their long flight from the Cold Maker to the Land of Sunshine.

So Cold Maker and Storm Bringer ride down out of the land where the Spirits dance, to take possession of Old Man's Garden for the moons of Frosts and Ice, to cover the land with a woolly white robe until Good-Old Man, the Chinook, rides once more out of the mountains on a rosy breeze.

INDEX